The Unconquered

PLATE I

THE STANDARD BEARER   [Photo. Fleming

From a miniature of Froissart's Chronicles.   British Museum, Harleian MS. 4379, fol. 104

[front.

The Unconquered Knight

A CHRONICLE OF THE DEEDS OF DON PERO NINO

Count of Buelna

BY HIS STANDARD-BEARER
GUTIERRE DIAZ DE GAMEZ
(1431-1449)

Translated and selected from *El Vitorial* by
JOAN EVANS, B.Litt., F.R. Hist.S.

THE BOYDELL PRESS

First published 1928
George Routledge & Sons Ltd

Reprinted 2004

first person singular

ISSN 1743-4769
ISBN 1 84383 101 5

The Boydell Press is an imprint of Boydell & Brewer Ltd
PO Box 9, Woodbridge, Suffolk IP12 3DF, UK
and of Boydell & Brewer Inc.
668 Mount Hope Avenue, Rochester, NY 14620, USA
website: www.boydellandbrewer.com

A CiP catalogue record for this book is available
from the British Library

Library of Congress Cataloging-in-Publication Data
applied for

This publication is printed on acid-free paper

Printed in Great Britain by
Antony Rowe Ltd, Chippenham, Wiltshire

CONTENTS

LIST OF ILLUSTRATIONS

LIST OF ILLUSTRATIONS

PREFACE

Gutierre Diaz de Gamez entered the service of Pero Niño, Count of Buelna, about 1402, when they were both some twenty-three years of age[1]. So long as his master lived, he served as the head of his military household, sharing in all his adventures and bearing his standard in all his battles. Nothing more is known of his personal history. After some thirty years of service, about 1431[2], he began a chronicle of his master's doings, *El Vitorial*, which he brings to an end soon after 1449.

His aim is frankly the glorification of his master. Pero Niño is perhaps hardly worthy to stand as the example of the perfect knight : his rashness, his occasional cruelty, a certain selfish irresponsibility can be read between the lines even of Gutierre's skilful and partisan narrative. Rather it is Gutierre himself, setting out to praise the master who is perfect in his eyes, who has achieved another end than that he strove for, in unwittingly showing himself as the perfect " loyal serviteur ", seeing only the best in his master, excusing, extenuating, advising, and defending him with sword and pen. Even his language, stilted enough when he is recording bookish and ideal things, unconsciously achieves new life and flexibility when he warms to his work of hero-worship, and describes action and danger and honour gained therein. He

[1] See Prologue, p. 14.
[2] At this date Pero Niño retired from party politics and thus from active strife.

ix

writes like a soldier, and by reason of his soldier-
liness can, for all the passage of the centuries, touch
ſtrings which ſtill sound to-day.

The chronicle seems, at all events, to have satisfied
Pero Niño, who, in his will executed in 1435, mentions
it in the epitaph deſtined for his tomb : " *Don Pedro
Niño Conde de Buelna, el qual por la misericordia de
Dios, mediante la Virgen Santa Maria su madre, fué
siempre Vencedor é nunca Vencido, por mar é por tierra,
segun su Hiſtoria cuenta mas largamente.*[1]" This same
will gives minute instruc̄tions for the cuſtody of the
manuscript of *El Vitorial*. It is to remain in the
hands of his widow for her life, and thereafter he
desires it to be kept in the coffer of the treasure in the
sacriſty of the Church of his town of Cigales, " *é que
non le saquen para ninguna parte ; pero quien quisiere
leer en él, mándo que dén lugar á ello* ".[2] In spite of
these precautions, the original manuscript has disappeared ; and some doubt exiſts whether these
inſtruc̄tions were ever carried out.

Several copies of the manuscript are recorded[3] and
four are known to survive. Don Eugenio de Llaguno
Amirola, the firſt editor of the *Vitorial*, used a single
manuscript that had once belonged to Don Aguſtin
de Montiano y Luyando, Direc̄tor perpetuo of the

---

[1] Llaguno, *Cronica de Don Pedro Niño*, p. 225. In the same will he leaves
Gamez the usufruc̄t of land worth 3,000 maravedis. As he is not mentioned in Pero
Niño's second will of 1453, we may assume that Gamez died between 1449 (when his
chronicle ends) and that date.

[2] *Ibid.* [3] Don José Pellicer de Ossau y Tovar in his *Informe del origen, anti-
guedad, calidad i sucesion de la . . . Casa de Sarmiento* (p. 63) mentions a
manuscript said to have been copied from that in the Church of Cigales, and
others seem to quote him without seeing the manuscript themselves. (Llaguno,
op. cit., p. IV.)

Real Academia de la Historia. He describes it as
written on 190 leaves of vellum, in a charter hand,
with blanks left for illuminated initials and ornaments,
decorated at the top of the first page with the arms
of the Niño family—or seven fleurs de lys azure—with
a patriarchal cross and hat above. Llaguno suggests[1]
that it was written for Don Fernando Niño, Patriarch
of the Indies and Bishop of Siguenza, who died in
1552. Professor W. J. Entwistle informs me that this
description corresponds to a manuscript in the Biblioteca Nacional of Madrid[2], which has marks in the
margin at all the passages omitted by Llaguno. The
manuscript is not complete; the copyist has left
lacunae whenever he encountered phrases or words
that he could not understand. On this manuscript
Llaguno based his edition of 1782[3], but he seriously
perverted it, and made many omissions without any
mention of the fact. Not even the beautiful printing
of his edition can disguise the fact that it is un-
satisfactory.

A second manuscript in is the *Biblioteca de la
Academia de Historia* at Madrid[4]. It is composed of
seventeen paper books, having in all 275 folios, written
towards the middle of the sixteenth century[5], in the
script called *letra formada castellana*. The margins
and initials are decorated with ornaments rather

[1] *Op. cit.*, p. vi.
[2] MS. 17648, formerly Gay. 209, from the collection of Pascual de
Gayangos, 1809-97.
[3] *Cronica de Don Pedro Niño, Conde de Buelna, por Gutierre Diez de Games su
Alferez*, Madrid, 1782.
[4] Est. 24 grad. 2a B, nro. 28.
[5] L. G. Lemcke, *Bruchstücke aus den noch ungedruckten Theilen des Vitorial von G.
Diez de Games*, Leipzig, 1863, gives it to the second half of the fifteenth century.

PREFACE

roughly executed in red and green ink. It fills up
certain *lacunae* in the Llaguno manuscript; but its
own gaps cannot be filled from the other[1]. Both are
derived from a common original. This manuscript,
collated with Llaguno's text, formed the basis of a
French translation published in 1867 by the Comte
Albert de Circourt and the Comte de Puymaigre.[2]
This edition is far more satisfactory than that of
Llaguno, and has been used as the basis of the present
edition. The English translation has then been
checked against Llaguno's Spanish text wherever
possible (while keeping nearly all the readings and the
fuller text of the French edition) since an English
phrase can often be found nearer to the Spanish than
any French construction can be.

Professor Entwistle informs me that he knows of
two other manuscripts of minor importance : one in
the Biblioteca Nacional[3], and one formerly in the
collection of Senor Menendez y Pelayo and now in the
Biblioteca Menendez Pelayo at Santander.

El Vitorial has provided several scholars with
material. The Spanish genealogists and historians
early made considerable use of it[4], and with Llaguno's
edition it became known outside Spain. One of
the first foreigners to draw material from it was
Robert Southey, who, in his *Lives of the British*

[1] Lemcke published from this MS. the stories of Julius Cæsar, Judith, the Legend
of the Palm-tree, and the account of Eleanor of Guienne, omitted by Llaguno.

[2] *Le Vitorial, Chronique de don Pedro Niño, Comte de Buelna, par Gutierre Diaz de
Gamez, son Alferez* (1379-1449) *traduit de l'espagnol d'après le manuscrit avec une
introduction et des Notes historiques.* Paris, 1867. It has long been out of print and
is difficult to obtain.

[3] MS. 5978; sixteenth- or seventeenth-century cursive hand on 68 folios of
paper; formerly Q 311. [4] See Llaguno, p. IV.

Admirals[1], gives a summary of such parts of the book as deal with Pero Niño's descents on England and Jersey. Another such summary, in French, was published by M. A. de Courson in 1854[2]. In 1868 Viollet le Duc included in his *Dictionnaire raisonné du mobilier* a translation by M. Mérimée into archaic French of the account of Pero Niño's visit to Serifontaine[3], while M. Jal made use of the descriptions of naval matters in the *Vitorial* to illustrate many passages in his *Glossaire Nautique*[4]. No critical edition of the Spanish text, however, has yet been produced ; and it is much to be hoped that one will soon be undertaken.

·　　·　　·

El Vitorial is a mirror of the complex age, at once decadent and fruitful, in which it was written. It comes at the end of the series of crusading narratives of which Villehardouin's is the earliest and Joinville's is the best ; and it is in some sort a prelude to the great Voyages of the sixteenth century. Pero Niño and his galleys are at the beginning of a Spanish tradition that ends with the Invincible Armada.

The ideal of Chivalry that Gamez expounds is often curiously at variance with the practice that he narrates ; yet it is the cherishing of this ideal, and the influence, however subtle, that it exercises on action, that makes *El Vitorial* a book definitely of the Middle Ages. Pero Niño is no Saint Louis : even in ideal he is not the humble servant of God, patiently working out his

[1] 1833 (Cabinet Cyclopædia), Vol. II, pp. 20-41.

[2] *Aventures et prouesses d'un capitaine caffillan et d'un chevalier français sur les côtes de Bretagne, Normandie, et Angleterre, en l'an de grâce* 1405, in *Annuaire du Morbihan pour l'année* 1854.

[3] Vol. I, p. 353.　[4] *Glossaire Nautique : Repertoire polyglotte de termes de marine anciens et modernes*, Paris, 1848-50.

purpose upon earth, with no thought of personal gain. God for him exists to help men in his difficulties, and to give him his desires in a world where, without heavenly aid, the odds would sometimes be heavy against him. He remembers God not at every moment, but only in a crisis, " since he could do nothing more, he prayed God to guide and guard his Christians."[1] The whole conception of chivalry was changing; to meet the seven champions of the White Lady in the tilt yard was as knightly an enterprise as any harrying of the Paynim on the Barbary coast. Moreover, artificial and romantic as it may seem, such an enterprise held all the seeds of Civil War. Yet Pero Niño's very rashness and foolhardiness mark him as belonging to a different age from that of Comines and Louis XI; and the endurance of hardships, the courage and the spirit of adventure that shine through the pages of the *Vitorial* perpetuate a tradition of heroism that is of no age or country, but universal and eternal.

.   .   .

The complexity of the fifteenth century is reflected in a curious diversity in the book itself. Its conventional disquisitions on chivalry and education (though lightened by first-hand observations), its lengthy borrowings from classic and biblical legend,[2] its debate between Wind and Fortune[3], its rather

[1] p. 80.

[2] The most interesting is the *Chronicle of England* (Circourt & Puymaigre, pp. 211-57), which appears to represent an otherwise unknown *Brut*. Professor Entwistle has transcribed it from the MS. and translated it, and may, I hope, publish it shortly.

[3] Circourt & Puymaigre, pp. 379-85.

clumsy and not too accurate accounts of contemporary history, are all part of a literary tradition that has its *longueurs* and is past its prime. But the actual narrative follows the free tradition of first-hand narration that is independent of bookish lore. Indeed, since my intention has been to offer in this edition such a selection from the *Vitorial* as would give the story of Pero Niño himself, the marked contrast between the two styles has made the task of selection almost automatic.[1] I have included a great part of Gamez' prologue, since it sets the note of chivalry for the story that follows: a story full of colour, adventure and romance, ranging in scene from Tunis to St Ives, and in subject from the boarding of a Corsair's ship to entertainment in a French country house. I have not scrupled to stop the narrative at the time of Pero Niño's marriage to Doña Beatriz; for one thing, the rest of the *Vitorial* is less personal in its narrative and less interesting in its events, and for another, it is better to remember Pero Niño unconquered and happy than to watch him fighting the enemies that he could not overthrow— Destiny, Old Age, and Death.

---

[1] I have omitted the chapter-headings, which vary in the two chief MSS. and appear in either case to be the work merely of the copyists. In the text a space indicates the end of a chapter, and three dots an omission.

THE UNCONQUERED KNIGHT

PROLOGUE

A T the beginning of every book, four matters should be sought out and examined; the material cause, the efficient cause, the formal intent and the final intent; for the hearer should seek and enquire who is the writer, of what matter he treats, how he would treat it and to what end and profit. The material cause is here the duty and art of chivalry; the efficient cause is He who inftituted chivalry; the formal intent is to celebrate the feats of a good knight and the final intent is the benefit of example.

First I would say what is the duty and art of chivalry; whence and for what reason it arose, and for the furtherance of what end was it founded; as likewise in what manner men began to be gentlefolk; for all these things were brought about by the dispensation of the Divine power, Whom it hath pleased so to order the world that there are therein three eftates of men : men who pray, men who fight, and men who labour[1]; and that each should follow his own calling.

. . .

By cultivation of the faculty of reason that God hath beftowed upon mankind more than upon any other creature to discern between good and evil, have men attained to the knowledge of the four cardinal virtues, which are Prudence, Justice, Temperance and Fortitude. These virtues are named cardinal, *a cardine*, the which is the hinge of a door ; for even as the door swings upon its hinges while remaining upright in its place, so should our human life be ruled by the four Cardinal Virtues.

In what manner should these virtues be defined ?

Justice is a habit of the mind, a judgment of the reason by which to each man is rendered that which is his. Thus, Justice is to accord to each man dignity and honour according to his due, lordship to whom lordship is due, tribute to whom tribute is due. Again, Justice is union in human fellowship, not to will evil to a neighbour, but to do him service; not to rob any man of his rights, but to restore to each man his due ; and to love God above all things.

Prudence is the discrimination of good and evil—to repel evil and to do good ; for man should know good from evil, should follow good and eschew evil. Prudence is then the distinction between good and evil, to choose the one and to flee the other.

Fortitude is to enter upon arduous tasks with as good a will as upon matters that are easy ; that you may not bow beneath adversity, nor be lifted up by prosperity. Again, fortitude is humility without pride or despair in prosperity as in adversity.

Temperance is the resistance to impulses of disorder.

Through Prudence have men come to the knowledge of the beginning of things and of their end, of that fulfilment which they should attain ; through Prudence they have discovered the cycle of the Seven

Liberal Arts of which men have great need for their life in this world. These Arts have they called liberal, since in old time they taught them only to children that were free-born ; they kept them hid from baſtards and from slaves. In another sense they are called liberal, in that they make us free of those things of which we have need, and deliver us from those which are harmful. And in Juſtice that renders to every man his own, have men found Mercy and Pity, that Juſtice may not overpass into cruelty, and that none may do to his neighbour as he would not be done by, but that he may do unto his neighbour the good that he would himself receive. In Temperance have men found Continence and Measure, to abſtain from the demands of desire, to look upon them with underſtanding, to weigh them in the balance of avarice[2], to make heavy the scale that ſtands too high, and to lighten that which swings too low, so that they may be equal as is fit ; to take of all things that which is needful and indispensable, and to leave that which might do injury, for desire likes and necessity drives. Fortitude teaches them to be firm and conſtant in a plan begun, to undertake heavy labours and to pursue them until they have attained their appointed end ; to speak the truth, to praĉtise it, to maintain it, and to be neither inconſtant or fickle in their deeds.

From among those who have lived according to the rule of these Virtues have risen those noble men who have endured to do great deeds whereof the fame has laſted after them in the world.

. . .

To form the estate of nobles, the people of the Law had one way, and the Gentiles another. The Gentiles sought for a way to choose out men for war. They deliberated after this manner, saying : " Let us take into battle those who practise the mechanic arts, such as stone-cutters, carpenters and smiths, who are accustomed to strike great blows, to break hard stones, to split hard wood and with great strength to soften iron which is very hard. Let us set them to the front in our battles ; they will strike mightily and give hard blows and with them shall we conquer our enemies." Thus did they, and armed them well and sent them into the fray ; and some were stifled in their armour, and some lost their strength through fear, and some took to flight, so that all their host were brought to defeat. Then the patriarchs said that it had been ill-planned ; rather should they send the butchers, who were cruel and accustomed to shedding blood without pity, men who slaughtered great bulls and strong beasts—" These will strike without mercy and without fear, and will avenge us upon our adversaries." They armed them well, and sent them into the forefront of the battle. But when they were there, their hearts failed them, and they also took to flight ; and it did not fall out as they had thought, but rather were they undone by this counsel. But there were also men who had fought well and who had not been among the chosen. Then the patriarchs decided when next they went into battle to set men on the heights who might see how the battle went, and might recognise those who fought with a good heart and struck good blows, and

4

gave not in to fear, and dreaded not death, but
ſtood ſteadfaſt.

Then when the battle was over, they took those
men, and gathered them together apart, and rendered
them thanks and great honour for that they had fought
so well. And they formed them into a hoſt apart,
and bade them do no other work but this, to maintain
their arms and tend their horses, and that all their
endeavour should be in those matters.

To maintain them, a tax was levied, and it was
found that this inſtitution was sound and good. All
the people honoured and loved them ; they named
them *omes de bien*, good men, the which gave them
heart to apply themselves to their work, and they
became the more cunning therein. When it befell
that one of them died in battle, men made great
mourning, and took his children and brought them
up in great honour, and gave them all that had been
their father's, making them follow the same way of
life as their father had followed, granting to them and
their mother the same privileges that the father had
enjoyed. And they called them *fijos de bien* and
continued to call them so. Afterwards the name was
changed and they were called *Fijos dalgo*, which likewise means son of a good man, son of a good house,
born of those who ever were good and did good.[3]
In the same manner those who fell into dishonour or
did some great villainy were called *fijo de ninguno*,
" no man's sons ".

As these chosen men were few in number, when they
went into battle each was given ten men to bear him
company, that his courage might impel the others to

do well; and indeed it often befell that through the valour and governance of a good knight a battle was gained or a strong place preserved or taken. Likewise they gathered together ten of those who were heads of ten and set over them one of the ten who was called centurion, for he was the head of a hundred. Then they took ten centurions, and chose among the chosen one of the best, whom they gave them as their ruler; and him they called *Miles* and Knight, for he was the head of a thousand. And then the Gentiles made a legionary, who was Duke and commanded six thousand six hundred and sixty men, which is a legion.

There was yet another manner by which knights were chosen.

Once it befell that Gideon went into battle, and went in great fear, for he had few men, and already he had seen cowards, poltroons, men without shame, taking to flight and bringing about the defeat of good men. He prayed God to shew him which men he should take with him into battle. Our Lord said to him : " On that day when thou goest into battle, it shall be very hot, for the sun shall strike straight and thy men shall be athirst. When thou comest to the river, mark thou those who shall drink with their mouths in the water; do thou leave those, take them not with thee, lead them not into the battle; but give heed to those who drink out of their hands; and these take thou into battle boldly."

These words are applied to gluttonous men without continence, who are never filled. They are as beasts who think of naught but what they shall eat. Even thus were those who had no shame to drink as beasts

6

drink and could not reſtrain themselves to drink as other men. He who has not command over his appetites, but lets them lead him aſtray, much less shall he have power to vanquish his enemies, but his small endurance shall make him to lose all shame and to sink into dishonour. So Gideon took with him those who had drunk from their hands, as being men guided by reason, and he went into battle, and he conquered. These men were set apart to serve him in battle and it is from among them that were made dukes, princes, counts, knights and gentlemen, who vow their bodies to do fair and mighty deeds, giving themselves to rough labours, enduring great fear and knowing how to reſtrain it by honour, and doing nothing that might be imputed to them for baseness. They were held to be so firm and true in word and deed to all those who treated them fairly that kings and mighty princes thought well to entruſt them with their wives, their children, their houses and their fortresses, on nothing but their word of truth, which is the pledging of faith and homage which they ask of gentlemen. To keep this faith, do good men bear hunger, thirſt, and anguish, do they let their wives and children suffer death, do they forsake them and die themselves if need be, to keep their word.

.   .   .

Since noble renown is a matter befitting knights and those who pursue the calling of War and the art of Chivalry, and not any others whatsoever, the writer indites this book for noble knights who ſtrive to win honour and renown in the art of arms and chivalry,

and to attain the palm of victory, saying to them :
" Take heed of those, Christian and Paynim, who have
endured so much to gain honour and renown ; and
so follow their example that ye lose not the lasting
joy, which is to see God in His glory, and therein to
dwell for ever in perfect felicity. Therefore take
examples from the faithful knights who have fought
for the Faith of Our Lord God. Take example from
Joshua, who gave battle so many times against the
Philistines, fighting for the cause of God with so
great a faith that God at his prayer stayed the sun in
its course and bade it not move until Joshua should
have had time to vanquish his enemies. Take example
also from King David, who, fighting for the Faith, by
his great faith slew Goliath the giant, and fought
other great battles. Take example also from Judas
Maccabæus who, after the destruction of the house
of God and of the City and of all the Jewish people,
withdrawing into the mountains of Caudio with few
folk, but with a great faith in God against his enemies,
seeing that his men were filled with fear to fight
against so great a multitude, said to them to give
them courage : ' The victory of battle standeth not
in the multitude of an host, and a small company is
not always overthrown by reason that it is a small
company ; but victory cometh to those who are loved
of God and fight with a single heart ' ". And he defied
the great army of King Antiochus, and Nicanor, and
Apollonius. Take example from Duke Godfrey of
Bouillon, who endured so many labours and gave
battle so often that he might conquer the Holy
Sepulchre and exalt the Faith, and especially when

with great faith he leapt from the bridge of his ship into the sea, wherefore he reached land before his enemies could come thither to hinder him. Take example from Charles Martel and from Charlemagne and from the noble kings of Leon, from the number of the great battles that they waged againſt the Moors and from their mighty deeds and from their gaining of the country where now we live. Take example from Count Fernan Gonzalez, beloved of God, who, fighting with faith and great courage, abased the might of Almanzor, and from the Cid Ruy Diaz, who, a knight of little account, but one fighting for faith, truth and the honour of his king and the realm, won many battles, and God gave him greatness and honour, and much was he feared by his neighbours. Take example also from the moſt noble king, Don Ferdinand the Chaſte, who, fighting for the Faith, conquered Cordova and Seville, where men honour him as a saint not canonized. All these have wrought the salvation of their souls, fighting in great faith againſt the Moors for the cause of Truth and leading a life of purity."[4]

.   .   .

Our Lord God has three orders of knighthood.

The firſt is the order of the angels who fought againſt Lucifer, when he would have exalted himself, and said, " I will set my seat on the side of the North Wind, and I will be the equal of the Moſt High." They fought againſt him and vanquished him, him and all his miniſters, and hurled them from the high seat of glory into the depths of the abyss. They ever wage war againſt them in our defence, and as guerdon of their valour, they bear the banner of the living God. Of this chivalry is St Michael chief, Archangel and Defender of the Church of God.

Our Lord God hath a second order of knighthood : of the Martyrs who have died for the Holy Catholic Faith, who have conquered the pomps, the temptations and the threats of the world, the flesh and the devil, who have suffered many torments and have died cruel deaths serving Jesus Chriſt and strengthening the faith ; they have been victorious and have attained the palm of victory and of martyrdom. Of these, Jesus Chriſt hath said, " To the victor will I give the crown and for guerdon shall I make him eat of the Tree of Life, that is in the paradise of my Father." They have won the crown and aureole.

Our Lord God has likewise other knights, who are the good kings of the earth, juſt, upright and God-fearing, and the good knights who vow to defend and protect our mother the Church, and the Holy Catholic Faith and the honour of their King and of the realm. For their recompense are those heavenly seats prepared for them in glory, that Lucifer and the evil angels loſt through pride. And see how *contraria a contrariis curantur* : these seats were loſt through pride, and it is by humility in victory that they are won by this order of knighthood of the good defenders. It has for head the Holy Virgin St Mary with all the saints and angels of the glory of Paradise.

Now is it fitting that I should tell what it is to be a knight : whence comes this name of knight, what manner of man a knight should be to have a right to be called a knight ; and what profit the good knight is to the country wherein he lives. I tell you that men call knight the man who, of cuſtom, rides upon a horse. He who, of cuſtom, rides upon another mount, is no knight ; but he who rides upon a horse is not for that reason a knight ; he only is rightly called a knight, who makes it his calling. Knights have not been chosen to ride an ass or a mule ; they have not been taken from among feeble or timid or cowardly souls, but from among men who are ſtrong and full of energy, bold and without fear ; and for this reason there is no other beaſt that so befits a knight as a good horse. Thus have horses been found that in the thick of battle have shewn themselves as loyal to their maſters as if they had been men. There are horses who are so strong, fiery, swift and faithful, that a brave man, mounted on a good horse, may do more in an hour of fighting than ten or mayhap a hundred could have done afoot. For this reason do men rightly call him knight.

What is required of a good knight ? That he should be noble. What means noble and nobility ? That the heart should be governed by the virtues. By what virtues ? By the four that I have already named. These four virtues are siſters and so bound up one with the other, that he who has one, has all, and he who lacks one, lacks the others also. So the virtuous knight should be wary and prudent, juſt in the doing of juſtice, continent and temperate, enduring and courageous ; and withal he must have great faith in God, hope of his Glory, that he may attain the guerdon of the good that he has done, and finally he muſt have charity and the love of his neighbour.

Of what profit is a good knight ? I tell you that
through good knights is the king and the kingdom
honoured, protected, feared and defended. I tell
you that the king, when he sends forth a good knight
with an army and entrusts him with a great emprise,
on sea or on land, has in him a pledge of victory. I
tell you that without good knights, the king is like
a man who has neither feet nor hands.

.   .   .

They are not all good knights who ride upon horses ;
neither are they all knights to whom kings give arms.
They have the name but they do not pursue the
calling. For since noble knighthood is of all offices
the most honourable, all men desire to be uplifted to
this honour ; they wear the mantle and bear the
name but they do not observe the rule of life. They are
not knights but phantoms and apostates.[5] The cowl
does not make the monk, but the monk the cowl.
Many are called and few chosen. There is not, and
there should in no wise be, among all estates, an estate
honoured as is this : since those of common and mean
estate eat their bread at ease ; they have soft garments
and savoury meats, easy and scented beds ; they go
to sleep in peace and arise without fear ; enjoy their
pleasures in fair houses with their wives and children
and with many men to do their will ; they become
thick-necked and paunchy ; they love their little
bodies and cherish them delicately and live in delight.
What guerdon or what honours do they deserve ?
None, nay, none. Knights who are at the wars eat
their bread in sorrow ; their ease is weariness and
sweat ; they have one good day after many bad ; they

are vowed to all manner of labour ; they are for ever swallowing their fear ; they expose themselves to every peril ; they give up their bodies to the adventure of life in death. Mouldy bread or biscuit, meat cooked or uncooked ; to-day enough to eat and to-morrow nothing, little or no wine, water from a pond or a butt, bad quarters, the shelter of a tent or branches, a bad bed, poor sleep with their armour ſtill on their backs, burdened with iron, the enemy an arrow-shot off. " Ware ! Who goes there ? To arms ! To arms ! " With the firſt drowsiness, an alarm ; at dawn, the trumpet. " To horse ! To horse ! Muſter ! Muſter ! " As look-outs, as sentinels, keeping watch by day and by night, fighting without cover, as foragers, as scouts,[6] guard after guard, duty after duty. " Here they come ! Here ! They are so many—No, not as many as that—This way— that—Come this side—Press them there—News ! News ! They come back hurt, they have prisoners— no, they bring none back. Let us go ! Let us go ! Give no ground ! On ! " Such is their calling ; a life of great fatigues, bereft of all ease. But there is no equal to the ill of those who make war upon the seas ; in a whole day should I not end my telling of their miseries and their labours. Great is the honour which knights deserve, and great the favour which kings should shew them, for all the reasons which I have told.

.   .   .

Reading then many hiſtories of kings and famous knights, I have found especially worthy of praise over and above any of them a moſt famous and illuſtrious knight, born in the kingdom of Castille, though his forbears came thither from France⁷ and were of the house of Anjou, which is one of the branches of the royal house of France. He gave all his life to the calling of arms and to the art of chivalry, and from his childhood laboured at no other matter. And though he was not in rank so great as those before mentioned, yet was he great by his virtues, and never was he vanquished by his enemies, neither he nor his men. Wherefore have I judged that he was well deserving of honour and renown, and worthy to be set by the side of those who have won guerdon and honour through feats of arms and of chivalry, striving that they might attain the palm of victory.

So that his noble actions might endure, have I, Gutierre Diez de Gamez, servant in the household of the Count Don Pero Niño, Count of Buelna, willed to set them down in writing, for I have seen the most part of the feats of chivalry and the fair exploits which this lord accomplished, being there present in person, for I have lived in his service since the time he was twenty-three years old, and I about the same age, more or less. I was one of those who marched regularly with him, and I had my share in his labours ; I ran the same dangers as he did and went through the same adventures in my time. To me did he entrust his banner : I had charge of it whensoever there was need. I bore him company in the seas of the Rising and the Setting Sun ; and I have seen all those things that here are written, and others that are too long to tell, all pertaining to chivalry, valiancy and courage ; of the which some were so noteworthy, that had it not been that God helped him, they could not have been performed by any man ; for he accomplished by himself feats of arms which a hundred men might not have brought to success, as you shall see later in the encounters I shall tell. Manifeſt was it that the especial grace of God was with him, since in none of the battles given or in any of the great adventures attempted did he ever turn his back to the enemy, nor was he ever beaten, neither he nor his men, in any work which they had to do ; but he was always victorious. Wherefore have I written of him in this book, which treats of his feats and his high adventures, as well in love as in war ; for, as he was in arms a man of good fortune, so was he in love very valiant and of good renown.

THE FIRST PART

THIS knight, Pero Niño, was of great nobility on both sides of his family. On his father's side he was descended from the royal house of France, from the branch of Anjou ; on his mother's side he belonged to one of the greateſt houses of Caſtille, which is that of the house of La Vega.

.   .   .

[1379] At the time when Doña Ines Laso was entruſted with the nourishing of the King Don Enrique, Pero Niño, her son, was a year and a half old. Thenceforward, he was brought up in the household of the king, and the king grew to have so great an affeċtion for him that he ever loved him more than any other of the children that were brought up with him.

.   .   .

When Pero Niño was ten years old, he was entruſted for his education to a wise and learned man, who instruċted him and taught him in all good habits and manners as befits a good and noble gentleman ; and this governor gave him such teaching as follows :

" My son, take heed that you are of moſt great and honourable lineage, but that the wheel of the world, which never is ſtill and never leaves matters well as they are, has brought it down from on high ; for it

17

2

is wont to make the great small, to throw into low estate and poverty those who have been set on high; and so it befits you to work and strive to return to this first estate, yea more, to excel in greatness and nobility those from whom you spring. That a man should equal his father in keeping the estate which he left to him, is no marvel; for he found this estate all won. But great praise is due to him when he excels those from whom he comes, and makes for himself a greater position.

" My son, pay great heed to my words, prepare your heart for my lessons and there treasure them, for later you shall have understanding of them. He who has to understand the practice of the art of chivalry cannot spend much time in the school of letters. What you know of such matters already is enough; what you lack, time will give you, if you apply yourself somewhat.

" Before all things know God; next, learn to know yourself; and then to know others. Know God through faith. What is faith? Faith is steadfastness, a firm and certain belief in something that has not been seen, an argument of the spirit, and a discourse of the intelligence that makes the essential known from its accidents. Know Him who has created you and given you being. Know God through His creatures, and through the marvels that He has wrought. Understand and know His great power; for He has made the heavens, the earth and all that therein is. He has created the angels in light; He has adorned and beautified the firmament with so many and such fair stars. He has created sun and moon, and has commanded the sun to shine by day and the moon to shine by night; He has beautified and increased the earth by so many and diverse plants, trees and herbs; and He has peopled it with beasts of so many and various countenances. He has set in the sea the great whales and many fish of divers kinds; and He has created birds and sent them forth upon the air. See how He has set limits to the sea and forbidden it to cross them, that it may not destroy the earth. My son, see how the sun rises in the east and sets in the west, and goes back to the point whence it came; and how the heavens, like the sea and the earth which rests upon the sea, and all things He has made, all obey Him and transgress neither His commands nor the limits which He has set for them in the beginning. Hear how He created man in His own image, and set him in the paradise of delight and bade him love Him and serve Him and fear Him, and obey His commandments, promising that he should live for ever in perfect joy and felicity and never die, and never know either pain or labour; how He set under the orders and power of man all that He had created on the earth and in the sea. And take heed how man, ill-fortuned creature, was deceived and sinned through weakness; for he transgressed the commandment of God, wherefore were the workings of Divine justice begun, which condemned him to death both in body and soul; and he was driven forth out of Paradise into the desert of this world, there to suffer and to die. Free as he had been, he became the subject and slave of Death, and has left us his children in this same slavery, bondmen of sin. My son, love and fear Him who has hurled from the heights of the heavens into the depths of the abyss, who has turned glory into torment, light into darkness and shadow, who has changed into Devil and Prince of Death that angel, so great, so beautiful and glorious, who dared to say in his pride : ' I will set my throne above the heavens on the side of the North Wind, and I will be the equal of the Moſt High.' Love Him who so loved us, that not only was He willing to take on our flesh, but humbled himself to the condition of a servant and suffered for us, and took our burden upon His shoulders, and delivered us and snatched us out of the power of the devil and out of the cruel domination in which we lived as subjeſts of sin.

"My dear son, have faith and ſteadfaſtly uphold all who believe and maintain our Mother, Holy Church. Let nothing draw you away from her nor shake your faith. What shall I say to you ? In the holy faith you were born and you have been made regenerate by the water of the Holy Spirit. If it ſhould befall that you muſt fight with your body alone againſt whomsoever would deny the Holy Catholic Faith, then muſt you do it ; for that is fair feat of chivalry, the faireſt that a knight can do, to fight for his law and his faith, above all things holding faſt to the Truth. If it hap that you fall into the hands of enemies of the Holy Catholic Faith, and they would make you deny it, prepare yourself to suffer every torment, howsoever great it be, that they may offer you ; and if you uphold and confess the Holy Faith of Jesus Chriſt unto death, in this holy conflict, as I have bid you, Death is called the victor, and it is the Slayer who is conquered. Take example from the knight St James,

who had his members cut off upwards from the fingers
of his hands and the toes of his feet, one by one so long
as any remained, and yet never could be brought to
deny Jesus Christ, but remained steadfast until the end
as a good knight should. There see a fair feat of
triumphant chivalry; there was won the aureole
crown that God promises to victors. Let no man say
in such a moment : ' Ah, death is a hard thing! I
will deny it now and do what they ask ; for, since I do
it under compulsion, I can abjure it when occasion
offers.' I tell you that he who gives in is not accounted
the victor, and that he who puts his foot in the net
cannot withdraw it when he will. It is in time of
trial that friends are known. If a man have firm
faith, in the hope of the reward the torments become
sweet. Think that the torment of Hell is harder than
the torment of the body. This is soon over, but the
pains of Hell endure for ever.

"What more shall I tell you, my son ? I will
bid you never to believe or to accept subtle arguments
against the faith. That which your mind understands
not and cannot attain to, believe, through faith ; for
if faith could be demonstrated would it cease to be a
virtue. God has not created you that you should
judge Him, but that you should obey His commandments. Know by how much God excels you. How
can a creature, bound and mortal, know the infinite
save through grace ? The Holy Catholic Faith has
been purified like gold which seven times has passed
through the furnace and each time comes out more
pure. What say I, seven times ? Nay, more than
seventy thousand times seven.

"My son, do all things with God ; keep His commandments, observe His precepts, respect His churches, honour His feasts and their mysteries ; then will He guard you and honour you. Entrust your affairs to Him ; ask much of Him, for all riches are His, and He will give you whatsoever is best for you. Have hope in Him. Without Him is nothing done, for whatever is done without Him is nullity and nothing ; and that which is done with Him lives and endures.

"My son, incline your ear to the petitions of the poor man ; listen to him, answer him in peace and kindness and give him alms. Deliver him who suffers under the hand of the proud. Make worthy prayer to God. Read books. Let His works be in your mind. Know that when we pray we speak to God, and when we read God speaks to us.

"My son, believe not those who promise to make you see and know your future. They will tell you that you will become a very great lord, that you will obtain this and that, and of all that they shall tell you, nothing will so befall. If you believe them, putting trust in vain things, you will waste the time that you should give to matters necessary to your honour and your affairs. But believe that God, who created you without your help, will guide you without your help. Take heed that you give no credence to false prophecies, like those of Merlin and the rest, and have no trust in them ; for, I tell you in truth, these things were invented and set in order by men adroit and skilful, to advance themselves in the favour of kings and great princes, to take from them the most they could, and to hold them in dependence with these vain imaginings, while they profited by their credulity. If you give heed you will see that with each new king there arises a new Merlin. He will predict that the king will cross the sea, destroy all the kingdoms of the Moors, win the Holy House and become emperor; and then we shall see that it all falls out as it pleases God. The same predictions have been made for past kings : the same will be made for kings to come. That which God has not willed to make known to His elect do sinners pretend to know. Yet all the true prophets have not prophesied save concerning the two comings of Jesus Christ, the first in poverty and humility, the last in majesty and power. Thenceforward have all been silent, for after the coming of Jesus Christ was there no further need for them. Merlin was a good man and very learned. He was not the child of the devil, as some say ; for the devil, who is a spirit, cannot ·beget sons, though well may he produce such things as come from sin, that being his function. He is incorporeal substance and cannot beget flesh. But with the great knowledge that he won, Merlin wished to know more than was fitting, and he was deceived by the devil, who caused him to see many things in order that he should repeat them. And among these things some proved true. It is, indeed, one of the habits of the devil, and likewise of any who would deceive, to advance some truth, so that they may be believed of him whom they would mislead. Thus, in the matters that concern England, did Merlin say some things in which some measure of truth has been found : but he failed in many others. And now all who would make predictions invent them and father them upon Merlin. But all things paſt, present and to come only exiſt in the presence of our Lord God. Who should know the will of God in things of the future ? Or should man know more in such matters than God ? It is false. Take heed that God has created a multitude of things, but that He has created nothing contrary to His power. See what Jesus Chriſt answered to His disciples, when they queſtioned Him on things to come, and on Anti-Chriſt : ' It is not meet that you should know the hour and the minute that God has appointed in His wisdom. Of one thing only may you be certain : that after summer comes winter : that you muſt prepare houses enclosed and warm, make ready ſtores of wood and victuals for the hard and unfruitful season in which you may not gather them : and likewise in winter should you make ready for summer.' Watch the sailor, who, during a fair wind, makes ready for a tempeſt, and in bad weather prepares for good, living in the hope of its return. That is good divination and a profitable knowledge of the future.

" Beware also, my son, of deceivers who promise to make you two doubloons out of one, to change ſtones into silver and copper into gold, who tell you that thus you may increase your possessions into a mighty sum, and become the moſt powerful personage of all your house and beſtow gifts and largesse, excelling your rivals and overcoming them. They will make deceitful experiments before you, to persuade you ; but if you employ their services, you will find yourself a poor man at the end, and your possessions all spent. I tell you that to profit by their calling, they seek out men of cupidity, with ill-balanced minds, who, after they have ruined themselves, are pointed at with the finger of mockery.

" Seek the company of good men, and you will be numbered among them. Beware of the company of evil doers, for without your perceiving it your nature will steal something from theirs. Be moderate in eating, drinking and sleeping. Do not give free rein to your appetite in things which may do you harm : he that knows not that appetite is the enemy of judgment is too near to the beasts. Plato says that we should not go according to our appetite, but against our appetite, for to go against our appetite is to follow a second impulse, which is good, for it pertains to the nature of the soul, mistress of the body and of the five senses. Then the body is restrained, ruled, held in by the soul that makes it clean and fair through fasting, prayer, chastity and good habits. If the body is given over to its appetites, it is given over to anger, lust, avarice, pride and other sins of an earthly nature, for earth governs the body as well as the other elements. On which matter Plato says : ' While thou art young, use thy understanding to change thyself, to make thyself clean ; prepare thyself altogether for the truth ; leave every lying thing, for it is of an earthy nature ; make thyself continent and prepare for the struggle ; keep far off from thyself all falseness and all sin, that are of earthy nature ; for the body, when it is too kindly entreated, turns its desires to corrupt things and by long habit craves for them so much that the soul cannot any longer be mistress of the imagination, and whether the soul agree or not, has to give consent.' This same Plato says likewise that the soul is to the body what the musician is to his instrument. If the instrument is out of tune, the musician cannot draw true notes therefrom, and if it is too far untuned it must be set aside, but when it is well tuned, the breath of the players fills it with harmony and it brings forth perfect and delightful notes.

"My son, give not up your noble person to the frequenting of ignoble women, for they love not and only desire to be loved. Their converse is shortening of life, corruption of virtue and transgression of the law of God and man.

"My son, when you have to speak before men, let your words be sharpened on the file of reflection ere they reach your tongue. Know that the tongue is as a tree, whose roots are in the heart and speech is its fruit : it reveals the heart openly. Take heed that while you speak others are sifting your words, even as you sift theirs when they speak. Say then only reasonable things ; otherwise it were better to hold your peace. Through speech is knowledge shewn : through understanding, wisdom : through words truth and learning, through works, steadfastness. If he who should not speak were silent and if he who should not hold his peace would speak, never would the truth be contested.

"My son, beware of avarice, if thou wouldst remain master of thyself ; otherwise shalt thou be a slave, for as the pile of riches increases, even so increases the amount of care. Mark well this : desire only that which thou canst have, if thou wouldst have that which thou desirest. Judge not a man by that which fortune has done for him; judge him by what wisdom and virtue there is in him. The honour that is derived from the possession of herds and raiment and steeds and metals, all things of earth, can it avail more than wisdom and virtue, that are things of the soul? Consider not thy vassals only for the profit that thou mayest draw from them, but hold them all as friends, and let them render thee that which thou mayest expect according to the law. Sweet words make love endure in the hearts of men; sweet words multiply friends and mollify enemies: a noble man has a gracious tongue. Mark that in time of prosperity many will protest their devotion to thee. Let thy counsellor be chosen as one out of a thousand. If thou findest a friend in fair weather, take him: but believe not in him over-lightly or over-quickly, since his friendship may change with the season. If he remain firm in his friendship after trial, look upon him as another self. Keep thine enemies far from thee: never cease to distrust them. So conduct thyself among men that if thou diest, they shall weep for thee, and if thou be absent, they shall long for thee. When thou seest a sick man with weakened mind, mock not at him, but ask thyself if thou art not of the same nature. If thou findest thyself in good health, give thanks to God. If ill hap befall thee, bear it, for thou art destined to go through all manner of fortune. He who says unpleasant things, hears that which pleases him not: be gracious to every man. There is no more noble thing than the heart of man: never willingly does he accept subjection. Thou wilt gain more men through love than through force or fear.

It is not courtesy to say behind a man's back what thou wouldst blush to say to his face.

"My son, mark four faults and be thou ware of them; they are Pride, Obstinacy, Haste and Sloth. The fruit of Pride is Hate; the fruit of Obstinacy is Quarrel; the fruit of Haste is Repentance; the fruit of Sloth is Ruin. All extremes are evil: avoid them; fear feareth all things and temerity undertaketh all things boldly.

"My son, serve the king and beware of him[8] : for he is like a lion who kills in play and overturns in frolic. Beware of entering the king's household when his affairs are disordered. He who plunges into the open sea when it is disturbed, it would be marvel were he to escape; how much the more if he plunge in when it is rough? My son, fear not death for its own sake; death is so certain that no men may avoid it, for we come into the world on condition of birth and death. He only should fear death who has done much evil and little good. Death is good for the good man, for he goes to receive the reward of his goodness; and good for the wicked man, for the earth is rid of his wickedness.

"I would not keep you longer for already the time draws near when you must shew what you are, whence you come, and where you would hope to go."

Thus was this noble youth brought up; and his gentle governor instructed and taught him until he was fourteen years old.

[1393] The king,[9] having reached his thirteenth

year and entering upon his fourteenth, was given possession of his realm. As it commonly happens that when kings are children and under guardians, there arise great divisions in the realm, that leagues are formed and that there is little juſtice, because the people have no one to fill them with fear, and that the great rebel, and do violence, usurp and commit outrage, so Count Don Alfonso, who was son of the dead king, Don Enrique, and was uncle to the King and was Lord of the moſt part of the Aſturias of Oviedo, had tyrannized, usurped, and formed leagues while the realm of Caſtille was governed by the King's Guardians. When he learned that the King ruled in his kingdom, and already began to do juſtice, he was filled with a great fear and fled into the Aſturias and eſtablished himself as a rebel at Gijon.

[1394] The King, so soon as he had knowledge of it, raised an army, marched againſt him and besieged him.

Gijon is a city on the coaſt of the Weſtern Sea surrounded by water. The wideſt entry thereto may be three hundred paces wide at low tide, and when the tide is high it is but half as wide. This tongue of earth is defended by a caſtle built upon great rocks againſt which the sea beats. Otherwise, all round the city is there nothing but rocks, rising into pinnacles and very high. On the side of the Caſtle, the Count had set boats to join the barrier, and when the sea was low the boats lay high and dry.

As soon as the King had eſtablished his camp, it was resolved to set out to burn these boats, and the next day at low tide a party of the King's men armed themselves to set forth to burn them. The noble youth Pero Niño knew that this enterprise was being undertaken and forthwith he went to the King and begged him as a favour to give him arms, for they were at war and in such a situation as demanded them and as yet he had none of his own. The King ordered his own arms to be given to Pero Niño. At this time the youth muſt have been about fifteen years old.

The men of the city, when they saw that their boats were to be burned, came out under arms in great multitude, and that day was there a great battle which laſted long. The noble youth fought so well and pressed forward before the reſt so often that none did so much with their hands as he. He ſtruck signal blows which drew blood from those who had ill-served his lord the King, and he was twice wounded. So long as the siege laſted, he thruſt himself forward so often and accomplished so many fair feats with his hands, that all spoke well of him and said that he had made a good beginning, and shewed a will to gain great honour in arms and chivalry.

.   .   .

[1396] While the King, Don Enrique, was before Gijon, news came to him that the Jewry of Seville had been sacked ; and this caused him to depart at once and to go thither. While he was at Seville, one day he had the fancy to go hunting in a warren near to the ford called the Ford of the Stockade. The huntsmen and his followers all went thither by land, and the King went in a little boat, going up the Quadalquiver on the flood tide to the place where he was to hunt. That day he dined at the Aljaba with the Count Don Juan Alfonso de Niebla; and then they all mounted. Then the pack came up and started a great boar, which plunged into the river, and the pack followed. The noble youth Pero Niño, who rode behind the hounds, went into the river after them, and reached the boar by swimming. He struck it in the water, thrust it through and bore it back to the land on the end of his spear, for all its struggles.

When the hunt was over, the King once more embarked, and with his men floated down stream to return to Seville. The current, strengthened by the ebb, was very strong; the oarsmen rowed with all their might: the boat had got much way on her. Suddenly, a heavy rope was seen barring the course down the river; it was the hawser of a net stretched across to catch shad. When they saw it, those who were with the king cried out, saying: " Saint Mary help us: for we are lost by that rope." But Pero Niño leapt briskly to the prow, drew his sword and gave it such a blow that he broke the hawser; it was thick as a man's knee, wherefore were all amazed. And the sailors said that with the speed at which they went, if the hawser had not been cut and if the boat had struck it, no man could have prevented the boat from overturning with the King and all on board. Behold two things worthy of mark for the honour of the noble youth: the good stroke of his sword and the presence of mind, by which the King and all who were with him were on this occasion saved from great jeopardy.

While the King stayed at Seville, there were held several jousts with lances of cane, in which the noble youth, each time that he shewed himself, was among the beſt. All those who there saw him can bear witness to the truth, if there were there any knight who so fairly thruſt a cane and ſtruck with such shrewd blows ; for more than one good targe was pierced by his hand, and but for the courtesy which he ever observed the canes he wielded might have caused many wounds. At other times they fought with bulls, and there was there no one who did such good service, as well afoot as mounted, awaiting them, exposing himself to great danger before them, thruſt-ing his lance boldly whether on foot or on horseback, and ſtriking such blows with his sword that all marvelled thereat.

[1396] Some few days later, the King departed from Seville, and went into Caſtille, where he learned that the Count Don Alfonso had not observed the covenants agreed between them ; he had indeed many grievances to bring againſt him. Therefore the King raised an army, set out once more againſt Gijon and laid siege to it a second time. The Count, perceiving the King eſtablished in his camp, boarded a ship that he had all prepared, and set sail for Bayonne in Gascony.

. . .

The city had a great garrison ; it was furnished with good arbaleſts fixed upon the ramparts, with many other inſtruments of war, with a ſtrong barricade outside the gates and with deep moats.

One day, the men of the army went to challenge at

PLATE II

THE ATTACK

[Photo. Catala

*From a miniature of the French translation of Livy. Paris, Bibliothèque de l'Arsenal,
MS. 5082, fol. 189*

[face p. 32

the barriers those of the Count's who had come out
against them. The youth Pero Niño diſtinguished
himself that day; he was one of those who thruſt
themselves forward the moſt and did beſt with their
hands. At the height of the engagement he had his
horse wounded; but he had borne himself so well
that day that thereafter men spoke much of him,
praising him and accounting him the peer of good
knights. And each day he so upheld his renown, that
whenever any man projeéted an emprise of arms, he
made much account of him.

Another day, some of the moſt adventurous youths
in the army among whom were Juan de Aſtúñiga,
Ruy Diaz de Mendoza, Pero Lopez de Ayala, and
others, having agreed together to attack with their
lances at the gate of the barricade, the youth Pero
Niño learned of their intent, and went to ask arms of
the King: then he donned them and went with the
others on foot. When they were come near to the
barricade he left them, and went forward alone to
the palisade againſt the tower which men call that of
Villaviciosa; and he crossed the moat with great
danger and toil of body, for he was within range of
the cross-bows of the city. The men of the city had
set all around their ramparts, and especially in this
place, planks ſtudded with sharp nails and covered with
earth, to run the assailants through. None the less
Pero Niño climbed the scarp, reached the barricade
and fought hard againſt those he found there, ſtriving
with all his might to break the palisade. There he
loſt his lance. He grasped his sword and received
many a blow from lance and axe and sword, yet

notwithstanding he succeeded in tearing out a stake from the palisade, and God be thanked, came very well out of this action.

Thereafter the city surrendered to the King, who had compassion on those that were therein. The King took the city and destroyed the fortifications. The Count, as I have said, was at Bayonne. The King broke camp and went to Leon. In this siege Pero Niño received many blows and wounds from lance, sword and other arms and there endured great toil.

[1396] But little time afterward there arose war with Portugal. The King of Castille assembled his army at Salamanca, and set it under the command of Don Ruy Lopez Davalos. At this time Pero Niño had already a household and men. The King gave him into the care of Don Ruy Lopez that he might take him with him, whereat Pero Niño was well content. Don Ruy Lopez had himself asked for him and he took him with him and ever bore him faithful company, and gained thereby good service in several matters wherewith he charged him.

Don Ruy Lopez set himself at the head of the King's army, went to Ciudad Rodrigo, and entered Portugal by way of the Alseda, burning and destroying as he went. He came before the city of Viseo and entered it by force. There he ordered Pero Niño to take command of the troops as they entered the city, and bade the troops follow him ; then he entered, slaying, sacking and burning the greater part of the city. And those that fled rushed into the Aseo, which is a fortified house, and there defended themselves. The King of Portugal was then at Coimbra, thirteen leagues from Viseo. This firſt campaign laſted seventeen days, during which Pero Niño never doffed his armour, at leaſt not that which a man may well bear every day. Coming into Portugal, he marched with the vanguard ; and leaving it, he kept in the rear.

.   .   .

[1397] Meanwhile, the King of Portugal besieged the city of Tuy, which is in Galicia. The King of Caſtille assembled the army again, and sent it againſt him under the leadership of Don Ruy Lopez Davalos. When they came to El Padron, the knights of Caſtille were no longer agreed, and if they had believed Pero Niño, young as he was, the city might have been succoured and would not have been loſt this time ; but they brought it no succour because they had behind them the Archbishop of Santiago, Don Juan Garcia Manrique, who had separated himself from the King, and after he had put himself in a ſtate of defence at Pontevedra, had caused other caſtles in this country of Galicia to revolt ; otherwise it would not have been taken. The army had to turn againſt Pontevedra, where was the Archbishop. A camp was pitched before the city, and on the morrow a fair troop of men at arms, crossbowmen and shield bearers,[10] came againſt the camp. Then was there a very close and perilous skirmish. Battle was given on a ground well chosen for those who would diſtinguish themselves in arms for love of their ladies ; for all the ladies and

35

damsels of Pontevedra were there to look on from the height of the city ramparts. Pero Niño came thither on horseback. His arms were a coat, a bassinet with gorget, according to the fashion of the time, leg pieces and a great tilting buckler which had been given him at Cordova as very fine, the which had belonged to the good knight Don Egas. The mellay was so close, and so thick the blows that were given on one side and the other, that it was ſtern to see. Even in the beginning of the battle Pero Niño had his horse wounded. He dismounted, set himself at the head of his men and advanced, offering and giving such ſtrong sword-ſtrokes, that those who found themselves face to face with him thought that they had to do not with a youth, but with a man robuſt and grown. Each of his blows was signal : from some did he shear a great part of their shields ; others did he ſtrike upon the head with his sword ; those beſt armed did he lay low upon the ground, or at leaſt make touch it with their hands, and by reason of their hurt leave their place empty as they withdrew to the rear. There, among those of the city, was there a famous foot-soldier named Gomez Domao, a very ſtrong man ; hardly did he press Pero Niño and weighty blows did he ſtrike. Well would Pero Niño have repaid them, but Gomez so made good use of his shield that he could not be touched. At length they came to grips one with the other and gave each other such sword blows upon the head, that Pero Niño averred that sparks flew from his eyes. But Pero Niño ſtruck Gomez so hard above the shield, that he split it for a hands-breadth and his head down to the eyes; and that was the end of Gomez Domao.

While Pero Niño was doing among the enemies of his lord the King as a wolf does among the sheep when there is no shepherd to defend them, it befell that an arrow ſtruck him in the neck. He received this wound at the beginning of the battle. The arrow had knit together his gorget and his neck; but such was his will to bring to a finish the enterprise that he had entered upon that he felt not his wound, or hardly at all; only it hindered him much in the movement of the upper part of his body. And this pricked him on the more to fight, so that in a few hours he had swept a path clean before him and had forced the enemy to withdraw over the bridge close againſt the city. Several lance ſtumps were ſtill in his shield, and it was that which hindered him moſt. When he had got so far, the people of the city, seeing the havoc that he wrought, fired many crossbows at him, even as folk worry a bull that rushes out into the middle of the ring. He went forward with his face uncovered and a great bolt there found its mark, piercing his noſtrils through moſt painfully, whereat he was dazed, but his daze laſted but little time. Soon he recovered himself, and the pain only made him press on more bitterly than ever. At the gate of the bridge there were ſteps; and Pero Niño found himself sorely beſtead when he had to climb them. There did he receive many sword blows on head and shoulders. At the laſt, he climbed them, cut himself a path and found himself so pressed againſt his enemies that sometimes they hit the bolt embedded in his nose, which made him suffer great pain. It happened even that one of them, seeking to cover himself, hit a great blow on the bolt with his shield and drove it further into his head.

Weariness brought the battle to an end on both sides. When Pero Niño went back, his good shield was tattered and all in pieces ; his sword had its gilded hilt almost broken and wrenched away and the blade was toothed like a saw and dyed with blood. And well do I think that until that day Pero Niño never had been able to glut himself in an hour with the toil he craved : for the truth is that the fight lasted for two whole hours, and that his armour was broken in several places by lance-heads, of which some had entered the flesh and drawn blood, although the coat was of great strength. It had been given him by a great lady; should I say by a queen, I should not lie.

No man should marvel that I should tell of so many feats done by this knight in so short a time, when he was still young in years ; for God endows all men with His grace and bestows His gifts on all, according to the measure that it pleases Him and the greatness of His mercy. To some does He grant the grace of being lettered, to others, that of being good merchants, to some to be good workmen, to others, to be labourers, and to yet others to be knights and good defenders. So, when the labourer would be a merchant, he loses his goods ; and the merchant, if he would be a labourer, understands nothing of his calling; and if he would practice chivalry he knows not how, for it is not in his nature. Likewise the labourer and the merchant, if they seek to follow the calling of letters, they know not how, for it is not in their nature. But to be brought up for chivalry and the calling of arms is a hard matter. It is for that reason that in knighthood more than one fails in his task, for he has not knowledge of the calling which he has undertaken. To one the plough will bring him more profit than the baldric ; to another the ink-horn more than arms. But the ſtudy and the work of this knight had never been for any other matter than arms, and the art and duty of knighthood ; and though he was beloved of the King and placed so near his person that many a time, if he had willed, he could have become his miniſter, yet since among miniſters there are of necessity found certain deceiving ways, and matters which spring not from the same root as chivalry, therefore would he never turn aside to such employment.

The King Don Enrique was moſt noble and moſt Catholic; he gave great honour to churches, and to the feaſts of God, St Mary, the Apoſtles, and the other saints. When the Church celebrated such a feſtival, he had prepared fair feaſts and processions, and furthermore ordered jouſts and tourneys and sports with canes ; then did he beſtow arms and horses, rich dresses and harness for those who should appear therein, and especially when there came to his court ambassadors of foreign princes. At his Court were many young and luſty knights who had good

underſtanding of these matters ; but this knight
Pero Niño shewed himself in these sports of arms
so able and so full of grace that it was marvel. Well
may I say that he alone unsaddled more knights than
all the other jouſters of Caſtille for fifty years ;
and the moſt of those he threw had overthrown
others.

This knight was fair to see, of a heavy build, neither
very tall nor yet short, and well-formed ; he had wide
shoulders, a deep cheſt, hips high on his body, thighs
thick and ſtrong, arms long and well made, thick
buttocks, a hard fiſt, a well-turned leg and a slim
delicate waiſt, that became him well. He had a low
and pleasant voice and lively and gracious speech.
He ever dressed well, with care and thought, making
the moſt of what he wore. A poor man's dress would
look better on him than the richeſt robes on many other
men. He had a better underſtanding of new fashions
than any tailor or robe-maker, so that the finely
dressed always took him as their pattern. In point of
armour he had much knowledge and underſtanding :
he himself used to shew the armourers the faireſt
shapes and tell them how they might make armour
lighter without loss of ſtrength. He was more learned
than any in the matters of swords and daggers and
bettered them much. As for saddles, no man of his
time underſtood them so well. He had them planed
down and ſtrengthened and at the same time had
the wood made thin and the trimmings and ſtraps

less. It was in his household that the divided girth, such as they use to-day, was firſt used. Of caparisons for jouſting he had more than any man in all Caſtille. He knew all about horses ; he sought for them, tended them and made much of them. In his time had no man in Caſtille so many good mounts ; he rode them and trained them to his liking, some for war, some for parade and others for jouſting. Hard did he ſtrike with his sword and ſtrong and signal blows did he make with its point ; never did he meet a man who cut and thruſt so well as he. He excelled in all other exercises which asked for boldness and nimbleness, in sports of lance-thruſting and dart-throwing. He was a mighty player at bowls and with the disc, as well as at hurling ſtones. He was also a mighty player with a spar and threw it better than other men ; in all these sports he was rarely surpassed by those who tried their ſtrength with him. Doubtless from time to time there may have been men who did one or other of these things in especial as well as he, this one one thing, and that another, but a man who did so well in them all generally, a man's body in which all these qualities were united, who accomplished all in such perfeſtion, was not found in Caſtille in his time. Moreover he used to bend the ſtrongeſt crossbows from the girdle[11] and drew as ſtraight an arrow with the arbaleſt as with the bow and never missed his aim. To see him shoot at a target with little quarrells[12] was a delight ; moreover, it was no marvel that this knight so far excelled the reſt in all such exercises, for, besides the ſtrong body and great force wherewith God had endowed him, all his care and all his means were

devoted to naught but to the calling of arms, the art
of chivalry and every noble labour.

God had been generous in giving him those virtues
of the soul that He divides among men. He was moſt
courteous and of gracious speech ; firm with the ſtrong,
gentle with the weak, gracious to all, prudent in
queſtion and reply, an upright judge and wont to
pardon freely. Gladly would he undertake to speak
for the poor, and to defend those who commended
themselves to his care, and he would help them from
his purse. Never did man or woman who asked an
alms of him go away empty-handed. He was true
and ſtaunch ; never did he break his word when he
had pledged it. He was always faithful to the King ;
never did he make treaty or league with any man to
the King's disservice, whether within or without the
realm. Ever did he labour to defend his King's
cause ; always did he hate and combat those who
rebelled againſt his King. He was firm and ſteadfaſt
in all his deeds ; never did he let himself be bought
by gifts or promises. He was ever liberal and never
prodigal ; never miserly and never grasping when he
should be giving. Never did he give himself up to
idleness and never did he waſte time that might be
spent in the honourable advancement of his affairs.
Temperance gave him his rule of life ; he was not
known to have any miſtresses in his youth, and likewise
never was he found eating and drinking except at the
fitting hours, for he knew the old proverb that says :

" Idleness, good fare, and honour never dwell in the same house."

Thus did this knight go on from ſtrength to ſtrength, in prowess and in well-doing, and thus was he diſtinguished among other knights as a palm tree is among other trees ; and his fair deeds made him so well eſteemed by Don Ruy Lopez Davalos that he would always have him with him in his chamber, at his table and in his council. Don Ruy had espoused Doña Elvira de Guevara, daughter of Don Beltran de Guevara. Doña Elvira had a siſter Doña Coſtanza de Guevara, who was the widow of Diego de Velasco, a great personage, brother of Juan de Velasco. Doña Coſtanza lived with her siſter ; and when Don Ruy Lopez dined, there were always four at table ; he, his wife, Pero Niño, and Doña Coſtanza. These laſt, by reason of this familiarity, came to fall in love, and their families coming to an agreement in the matter they were betrothed, and their wedding celebrated with much magnificence. Doña Coſtanza was beautiful, rich and of good lineage. She gave him a son, who was called Don Pedro. He was a fair lad, well nurtured, who in all his ways bore a great likeness to his father and gained men's eſteem by his deeds as well as by his good qualities. He entered the King's household, where he won the love of the King and all the Court. He shewed himself often at the jouſts and at other scenes of honour, as befits a man of gentle birth. An illness befell him which grieved his friends mightily ; it lasted long, and then carried him off at the age of twenty-seven.

Doña Costanza lived four or five years wedded to Pero Niño and then she died.

But since the marriage of Pero Niño and Doña Costanza was a work of love, and since this knight, just as he was valiant and excelled in arms and chivalry all the other knights of his day, so did he distinguish himself by setting his affections high ; and likewise just as he brought to a fair end all the emprises of arms that he entered upon, and was never vanquished, so wherever he loved was he loved in return, and yet never incurred reproach by reason of it, therefore will I treat here somewhat concerning Love and the art of Loving.

It was in the nature of things and befitted a youth so accomplished, who had shewn so much prowess, who was so much praised by all men, to have early knowledge of love. We know that men of this sort are spoken of with praise in the households of queens and of ladies, that they are well considered there and can gain hearts easily ; for fair and gentle ladies, such as are worthy of love, think to have gained honour when they know that they are loved by such men and praised of them. Likewise they know that for love of them do they become better knights and acquit themselves more magnificently, that they achieve prowess and great labours of chivalry, whether in arms or in sports, that they set forth on great adventures

to do them pleasure, and go into strange realms bearing
their devices, seeking chance encounters and encounters
in the lists, each praising and exalting his lady and
mistress. Moreover, they make about their ladies and
for love of them, gracious songs, most pleasant declara-
tions, notable sayings, ballads, songs, roundelays, lays,
virelays, complaints, tales of dreams and sonnets, and
allegories[13] where each declares himself in words and
makes the most of his passion. Others who dare not
so declare themselves, disguise their love and praise her
in emblem ; but they shew that they love in high
places and are loved in return, choosing at their fancy
the manner of making this evident. Over and above
all this it must be said that every lady desires to have
for betrothed and husband and lover the best and the
most gentle ; if they were let to have their way or if
it lay in their power, some of them would choose
husbands more to their liking, more gentle and of
better character than are those who are given them,
because love seeks not great riches nor great estate,
but a man brave and bold, true and loyal. Thus did
this lady Doña Costanza love and choose such a man,
thinking that her good fortune had sent him to her.

This marriage, then, having been made for love,
I will here treat somewhat concerning love, and will
shew what manner of thing it be.

Love is union of two beings of whom one loves the
other or desires possession of the other. I find that
there are three degrees in love. The first, I call
attraction ; the second, predilection ; the third,
devotion.[14] Let us speak of a lady who loves a knight
whom she has never seen. She hears tell so much of

45

the goodness and nobility of this knight, that without seeing him, she loves him and desires to see him and disturbs herself much to have sight of him. And after she has seen him, she finds that there is in him more goodness than ever she had heard tell, so much does she find in him. Henceforward she loves him more, and there is borne in her heart such an affection and such a predilection that already she would that she were united to him, and that she had him whom she loves so well for her own. Wherefore she takes pains to gain him whom she loves so much, until he shall have given up his will to hers and submitted himself to her. Thereafter when she holds this knight in her power, she has full knowledge of his worth and loves him so passionately that she cannot rest an hour without him and must always have him as she wills to be content ; she prizes him so high that she loves him as herself and even more than herself ; and if by chance it happen that he is separated from her, seeing him no more, she is ready to die for him ; and it sometimes befalls that she does indeed die, giving herself up to death for his sake. This is devotion, which is the highest degree of love.

.   .   .

Doña Costanza was then young and widowed, beautiful and of high lineage. It lay in her power to marry whom she would and she had determined in her heart what manner of man she would espouse. She had heard many gallant things told of this knight, young, fair, generous, bold, courageous, gentle and in all things as he should be, so that everyone made mention thereof. Reason, and God, who guides all good things, led her to choose such a man, whereat all her friends and family were content, approving the marriage ; and with him was she honoured so long as she lived.

.   .   .

[1397] The King of Portugal besieged the city of Alcántara and eſtablished his camp round about the city in such wise that he altogether surrounded and blockaded it, except for the river and the bridge that could not be blockaded. The King Don Enrique sent his army againſt him, under the Conſtable Don Ruy Lopez Davalos, with few enough men. He took up his position beyond the bridge, and any man who liked might enter or go out from the city and the camp. One day the Conſtable brought out thirty light horsemen and sent them againſt the Portuguese camp, between the hill and the river upſtream, towards Las Brozas. Behind them he sent as many as a hundred men at arms on foot and as many crossbowmen and foot soldiers in support of the horsemen, who, when they saw that they were supported, went to attack within the camp. There were there Ruy Diaz, his brother Mendoza, Pero Niño, and other good knights. A great troop came out of the Portuguese camp againſt them and they were engaged in a very close skirmish. The Caſtillians stood firm ; many of them were already wounded ; Pero Niño was hit twice in the legs, once with a lance and once with an arrow. His men bore him back to his tent. The Caſtillians were on the low ground and the Portuguese ſtill held the heights. If Pero Niño had not been wounded early, his ardour could not have failed to kill him or to leave

47

him prisoner. So long as he was in the battle the Castillians did not give ground ; but when he was gone, they were forced to turn and to go down again along the river, close against the cliff which is there very high. Many went back more by force than willingly, and so all came ill-ordered. At that point the good knight, Ruy Diaz de Mendoza, who had stopped near a hermitage, came back to them with some more of his men and gave new heart to this rabble, and stopped them, like the good knight he was. The Portuguese got no further, for they were already within range of the town, and each day after there was some pretty skirmishing with them. Each day Pero Niño was there and did as much as any man. The Constable would willingly have given battle, but there was no ground to deploy his troops. None the less they did so well piecemeal that the King ended by raising the siege and went back again to Portugal. Our men let him go, for the most part of the Castillians had not yet come, and the King of Castille sent for the Constable and all his men.

[1398] The next year the King Don Enrique assembled his army and sent it into Portugal under the command of the Constable, Don Ruy Lopez Davalos, who, at his entry, besieged Peñamocór and took it by main force. There did a good knight die, a kinsman of the Constable's ; he was named Lope de Sotomayor. Don Pero Lopez de Ayala was wounded by a block of stone which hit him on the helmet, while he was bravely acquitting himself of his knightly duty; thereof did he later run great risk of death. Pero Niño was in this expedition and did as well as any man therein. When he had taken Peñamocór, the Conſtable went thence to set siege to Miranda. There it befell that a party of our men came close to fight againſt the men of the city, the citizens of Miranda being assembled on the round of the ramparts, which were rather low. Pero Niño found himself there, armed with a coat of mail, a helmet and a shield, and began to hurl ſtones againſt those who were the other side of the bulwarks. He was as skilled in this sport at any man can be; with a throwing-ſtone, but of uncommon size, he ſtruck a man who shewed himself between the battlements on the helmet, and in the judgment of many witnesses, the man was seen to fall backwards. While the siege laſted Pero Niño did many other deeds which put his boldness to the teſt while fighting according to his wont.

HERE ENDS THE FIRST PART

4

THE SECOND PART

THE Second Part treats of the second age of Pero Niño,
when he had come to the age of his manhood, which
is after the twenty-fifth year. So long as he was
accounted a youth, from the time when he could bear
arms, he had always remained under the governance
of the Constable as the King had commanded him ;
then the King, seeing that he was of an age and
capacity to govern himself and others, set men under
his command.

[1404] At this time the King received many plaints
against powerful Corsairs, of Castillian birth, who went
about in the seas of the Levant, plundering men of
Castille as well as foreigners. The King, being much
vexed thereat, called Pero Niño, and very secretly
gave him charge of this matter, for the which he
ordered him to man galleys at Seville, with power to
choose whatever he needed. The King was noble in
all that he did ; he commanded that for this armament
they should choose the best mariners, experienced in
the navigation of galleys, that could be found in
Seville, as well as sturdy oarsmen, brought up to the
sea and stout of heart ;[15] that the best crossbowmen
should be sought for, men well knowing the handling
of their arms, good marksmen and trained to bend the
arbalest from the girdle ; and likewise that in all the
lagoons of Seville they should seek out quartermasters

and rowers, both for the forward and the backward ſtroke,[16] the beſt that there were, and that they should all be chosen among men who were born of that country, so that they might be assured of their faithfulness and loyalty. The King had them paid in advance, both Pero Niño and the men, their full wage for all the time of their service according to the usage of Caſtille. Moreover, he furnished Pero Niño with great quantity of arms, of good and very ſtrong arbaleſts, and he provided him with money, both gold and silver, to spend in foreign lands. Pero Niño took with him his cousin, Fernando Niño, and up to thirty men at arms, men of gentle birth of his own age, brave, ſtrong and well armed. More could not go in the galleys, but others went in a sailing ship[17] that the King had given him, that was commanded by Pero Sanchez de Laredo. When the galleys were equipped and all their needs furnished, Pero Niño held a muſter of them according to the usage ; and all those who had seen many galleys declared that never had there been so fair a muſter and so ſtrong of such a number of galleys. They all prayed to God to grant them fair weather and fair fortune. He had for maſter of the ships[18] and counsellor, an old knight, Micer Nicholas Bonel by name, a Genoese, with much knowledge of the sea and a good mariner, who had been maſter of galleys and had taken part in other great affairs, and Juan Bueno of Seville, maſter of the oarsmen,[19] the beſt and sureſt officer of galleys in all Spain.

When Pero Niño had taken counsel of the captain of the ships and the maſters of the oarsmen, they began

to row and the galleys passed beyond Coria. There
was a man of Seville, much honoured, who seeing this
fair muſter and the resolution for noble deeds which
was evident in the captain and his men, moſt earneſtly
begged Pero Niño to make some ſtay at his house,
where he would find a good reception. Pero Niño
granted this for love of certain knights of Seville who
came with him as far as Coria. Therefore they landed
for dinner, Pero Niño, the knights who came with him,
and all his gentlemen. You may imagine what
manner of banquet it was at which so great and noble
a company took their places. Neither food in abundance and diversity nor inſtruments of music nor talk
of war and love was lacking. At the end of the meal
a roaſt peacock was brought in, fairly served with all
its tail of feathers, and the maſter of the house said :
" I see here a moſt noble company who all purpose
good deeds ; I see likewise that my lord the captain
and all his gentlemen are in love. Love is a virtue
which pricks on and suſtains those who seek to prove
themselves worthy by feats of arms. Therefore, in
order that we may see who beſt loves his lady, and has
the firmeſt purpose to do good deeds, let the Captain
and all his gentlemen, for the greater honour of the
feaſt, boldly make a vow, each one according to his
courage and eſtate."[20]

Whereat all the company were joyful and content,
and even those who had some underſtanding of these
matters were full of admiration therefor. I will not
write here all the vows that were made, for it would
be long to recount them, but I will tell you that the
Captain led his men to places where each could well

find the means to fulfil his vow, as indeed the moſt of them did.

The galleys left Coria, reached Barrameda, and then Cadiz. Thence passing Sancto-Petro, they entered the Strait of Gibraltar and arrived at the city of Tarifa, where was the good knight, Martin Fernandez Puertocarrero. There Pero Niño received a fair welcome and all his men likewise. When they left there they went to caſt anchor that night in the mouth of the river Guademecil. On the morrow they appeared before Gibraltar and Algeciras ; there many Moors afoot and on horseback came to have sight of the galleys, and a Moorish knight embarked on a *zabra*[21] and came to beg the captain to bring the galleys before Gibraltar, and they would offer him the *Adiafa*, which means a present ; for there was at that time a truce between them and Caſtille. The Captain did so, and they brought him cows, sheep, fowls, abundance of baked bread and great flat plates[22] full of kouss-kouss and other spiced meats; not that the Captain would touch any of the things that the Moors gave him. They made there great entertainments of dances, with flutes, trumpets and other instruments.

The Captain then left Gibraltar, passed before Almuñeçar and touched at Malaga. This is a city fair to behold, in a good position in a plain. On one side the sea comes close to the walls, leaving between them and it a sandy beach which may be twenty or thirty paces long. On the weſt is the dockyard,[23] which the sea washes and even surrounds ; on the north, towards Caſtille, lies the city, a little raised on a small hill. It has two *alcazares*, or caſtles, separated

one from the other. There befell a thing amazing to
those who had not seen the like ; that is, that while
the galleys were being rowed along the coaſt, as much
as two miles from Malaga, with a calm sea, the sun in
the south weſt, the month of May half run, there
suddenly arose a thick fog, which coming from the
direction of the city enwrapped the galleys in such a
darkness that no man could see from one to the other,
although they were very close. And certain sailors
who had witnessed this thing before said that the
Moors wrought such appearances by means of spells
and did it that the galleys might be loſt ; and that
the oarsmen muſt be unbound, in case they ſtruck a
rock ; but that all muſt make the sign of the cross,
and make prayer to God that He might deliver them
from this spell, which would not laſt, but would at
once vanish. And indeed, as soon as they had said
the prayer, the fog dispersed all of a sudden and utterly
vanished and the sky was once more clear. They took
to their oars again and at once there came up another
fog like the firſt ; and again they prayed and again it
disappeared suddenly as before. The spell laſted for
about half an hour each time. Then the galleys came
before Malaga, everyone in arms on deck, each well
armed and ready for the fight, if need were. Many
Moors, both men and women, came out of Malaga to
see the galleys and soon a *zabra* came alongside with
Moors of authority therein, come to ask what meant
this armament. They saluted the Captain with respect
and begged him to wait, promising him the *adiafa*,
but asking that he should give his word not to attack
the port, the which he gave. Then as many as

five hundred knights came out of Malaga, mounted on good horses, with war harness well appointed, and began to wheel and manœuvre very bravely and in good order. The Captain said that never yet had he seen a troop of Moors whose looks he liked so well, and that it would better have pleased him to be facing them with three hundred Chriſtian knights, than to be there eating the *adiafa ;* and that if it had not been for their truce with Caſtille, he would have gone ashore and tried their worth. That night they brought the *adiafa* moſt honourably on many *zabras* decked out with tapeſtries of silk and gold, to the sound of cymbals²⁴ and other inſtruments. Those of our men who wished went into the city, where they were entertained in the house of the Genoese, and went to visit the Jewry, as well as the dockyard.

During the night the Barbary wind began to blow, which is an evil wind on that coaſt ; for the harbourage of Malaga, which is open roads, is not sheltered from all the winds. Our men returned on board the galleys to spend the night, and before the break of day they put to sea, making for Cartagena. At the hour of prime the wind veered to the weſt, blowing aſtern, and blew hard, so that the sea taught what manner of thing it was to the untried mariners. All day the galleys ran under their ſtorm trysails,²⁵ tossed by the gale towards Almeria, and with great difficulty were they able to reach the port of Las Aguilas by evening. There did they pass the night and the next day came into the great and secure harbour of Cartagena, where the crews refreshed themselves and repaired the damage which the galleys had suffered during the gale. Then, when they had held a council, they took to the open sea in search of Moorish ships.

At daybreak, a great sailing ship was sighted off Barbary, and the galleys steered for her ; but she was so far off that before they could reach her she had gained the coast and was in safety.

The galleys thus cruised along the coast of Barbary, seeking for Moorish ships, and encountering none. The captain then told his ship-masters that he would like to see what manner of men were those of Barbary. It was resolved to go to get fresh water at certain springs called the Caves of Alcocevar, which are by the sea shore and in a place surrounded by heights, so that it is easy to prevent anyone watering there. As soon as the captain had examined the position he understood this and said to his men : " I see what manner of country this is ; if we do not seize the heights there at once we cannot take in water without great harm befalling us." The ship-masters begged him for pity's sake not to land, neither he nor any of his men, saying that the Moors of this place were accustomed to war, by reason of the great number of Christian ships that frequent that coast, and that already they shewed themselves in force upon the shore. The custom of these Moors is to prepare ambuscades in secret places ; wherefore many Christians, not knowing how to protect themselves, have fallen into misadventure. But the captain answered : " Either we must give up taking in water, of which we are in great need, or we muſt take the heights; for if we take it in otherwise, we shall come to much harm and may even be driven to leave the place againſt our will." Then he took as many men as seemed to him sufficient and climbed with great effort and danger the ſteep cliff of the heights, on which he set his banner, to ſtay ſteadfaſtly there, arraying round it twenty shield-bearers with cross-bowmen behind, who shot without intermission. Nevertheless the number of the Moors increased every moment; they thruſt forward, then pretended to take to flight, then came back to the confliƈt, then turned their backs. The captain underſtood that they had an ambuscade, but that it was at some diſtance, and that they manœuvred thus to draw them away from the shore. He spoke to his men and told them to charge the Moors all at once and with one heart, since it was not a time for delay. All then, and he with them, ſtruck so hotly at the midſt of the enemy, that in this attack they overthrew a great number; for the Moors of this country are very lightly armed, which does not prevent them from being bold and fighting well with the few arms they bear. The reſt took to flight. The captain came back to the galleys safely with his men, and found that in the meanwhile they had taken in as much water as they needed. As for the Moors that had been beaten, they marvelled at the gallant men they had seen that day, and several of them swam out to sea to reach the galleys, crying out that they wished to become Chriſtians, and so they did.

Thereafter the galleys coaſted for several days along

the shores of Barbary, and searched the Habiba Islands ; but as they encountered no Moorish ships, they returned to Cartagena.

After his return from Barbary, while he was at Cartagena, the captain had news of a Corsair who gave great displeasure to his lord the King. This was Juan de Castrillo, who with Pero Lobete had slain Diego de Rojas, a man of high estate and noble lineage. They had treacherously slain him on a road where he was journeying without fear; and Juan de Castrillo had then become a Corsair, and went about the seas despoiling all he met, with a galley given him by Juan Gonzalez de Moranza, a knight of Castillian birth, who lived at Naples. Another Corsair, named Arnaimar, scoured the seas in concert with him on another galley. The captain learned that they were off the coast of Aragon, doing much harm, and he at once set out. He went to seek them first at the Cape of Palos, then at the Cape of St Martin, then at Blanes, Barcelona and San Felió, and so from place to place until he had news that they were round about Marseilles.

At this time the Pope Benedict[26] was at Marseilles, lodged outside the city in a Benedictine monastery called St Victor, which is set above the sea. Marseilles is a town built on a little round mountain, along the slopes of the mountain, going down as far as the plain. It is well shut in on every side, except on the side of the Port, where the walls end. The sea comes right

into the ſtreets, which have raised causeways. The
harbour is sheltered from all the winds. A ſtrong
chain of iron closes or frees the entrance, which is
very narrow. This chain is riveted to a great light-
house in the middle of the harbour, so that no ship
can come in or go out without leave.

The two Corsairs were there under the protećtion
of the Pope, drawing pay from him. They used to
go out to plunder and come back to Marseilles. Before
the Port are islands, of which one is called Pomègues,
where there is always a lookout with a flagſtaff rigged,
which has two courses ; one a sail of a ship and the
other the sail of a galley. The ship-sail is wide and
square ; the galley-sail wide and three-cornered. The
lookout keeps watch, and at each ship that he sees
coming in from the sea, he lowers one of the sails,
according to the kind of vessel.

As soon as he sighted the captain's galleys, he
signalled them, and the Corsairs made ready, not
knowing who it might be ; for if they had known that
it was the captain, they would not have waited even
to sight him ; I know well that they had no great
wish to encounter him. While the captain's galleys
were ſtill running for the Port of Marseilles, when they
had doubled one of the islands, we saw the Corsairs,
their hands on the oars and their course set for the
open. We ceased rowing to hold a council, according
to the cuſtom. At this moment what we feared was
that they would get away, and not that they would
await us ; but they, seeing that they could not make
their escape, had recourse to a manœuvre that profited
them much. They made as if they wished to fight

and gave out arms from hand to hand down the oarsmen's gangway, as if everyone were arming. Our captain was warned that the other galleys were arming, and told that it was ill for unarmed men to fight armed men; and ordered us to arm on the upper deck. The others, like true Corsairs, watched closely all that was going on. As soon as they saw that all the captain's men were armed, while they had laid down their arms, they all turned and made off.

Now any man of understanding will see that an unarmed man moves more swiftly than an armed man, and that he is the freer to row; and that similarly a galley whose crew is in arms on the deck will be much hampered in giving chase or being chased. The captain's galleys took to their oars again as soon as they had made out the manœuvres of the Corsairs. These, in spite of their speed, did not dare make for the open sea, but strove with all their might to get within the harbour of Marseilles, which was about two miles off. The captain's galleys came behind them eagerly, like men who see a great booty before them. The captain's galley rowed so hard that it was wonderful to see; but the harbour, which was so near, succoured the Corsairs when they had great need of it, for already we were within earshot one from the other. During all this time, the quarrells sped from one ship to the other.

Then another of the Pope's galleys came out of the Port, in which came knights of great estate, and all the boats and vessels which were in the harbour were manned, among which were more than twenty boats for coral-fishing manned by Genoese.[27] The sailors maintained that we should not wait for so many; that there were enough of them to fight five galleys; and the captain answered : " How shall it be known that we are better men than they, and are made for greater matters, if we do not wait for them ? " Then he said to his cousin, Fernando Niño, mafter of the second galley: " Do you follow me ; I will go firft. Two galleys will grapple me ; do you grapple the third, and if you have finished firft with yours, come to my help ; I will do as much for you if I am firft rid of my two." And he said to his men : " Men of Caftille, take good heed where we are, how that you have upon you this day the eyes of men belonging to all the nations of Chriftendom, and that we muft win honour for Caftille where we were born, and for ourselves. Fight fteadily. Let not a single one of you be taken prisoner, for he who is captured will not escape death for that. With the help of God and by His juftice shall they be beaten, for they are robbers and evil doers : they shall not endure before us."

The Pope and all those that were with him in his tower looked on at what was happening. The Corsairs' galleys were at this moment hugging the land at the entrance to the harbour, and, well knowing the boldness and the gallantry of the captain and his men, never did they dare come away from the shore. The captain, hoping that since they were now so many they might come againft him, had all things in readiness for battle.

Meanwhile, they sent out a brigantine, on board which came a knight of St John of Jerusalem, who asked whence came the galleys and who was their

captain ? They answered him : and then they asked
what were these other galleys and why they did not
come forth ; and he said that these galleys were there
under the safeguard of the Pope. Then the knight
returned to the city, and after a little time came back
in the same manner, and told the captain that the
Pope sent him his blessing, asking and commanding
him in virtue of his obedience to promise to keep the
peace in his Port, and not to do any hurt to these
galleys, and to respect all that pertained to him, and
that in consideration of this he should have his full
blessing and receive a fair welcome. When the captain
saw that for the present he could do nothing more,
that the Corsairs were so situated that there was no
way of taking the advantage of them, he ordered his
men all to say that they had mistaken them for Moors,
and that for this reason they had wished to seize them.
For himself, he told the knight that he commended
himself to his Holiness the Pope, for the love of whom
he would safeguard the galleys and all things that
pertained to him, but that for many reasons he had
need to enter the harbour. The knight went back
very joyful to the Pope and was not long in returning.
This time he told the captain that the Pope sent him
to invite him to enter the harbour with his galleys and
to come and see him. The captain accepted. At
once they hoisted the standards on all the galleys and
gave the salute, as is the custom of galleys when they
encounter friends. The Pope's galley entered the
harbour first, the captain after her and the other
galleys following. So great was the triumph that day
for the Castillians who climbed the Pope's tower that it

passes description. Barques and brigantines, great
and small, as many as there were, full of people, came
to see the captain and his men. Refreshments were
brought to them, bread, wine, meat in abundance,
and fruit, all that could be found. The captain landed
and was well received by the knights of the court.
He went to see the Pope, from whom, as from the
cardinals and great personages in his company, he
received fair welcome. The feaſt of St John the
Baptiſt fell in this week; the Pope celebrated it
solemnly and said high mass. He held a court[28] and
gave a feaſt to which Pero Niño was bidden. The
Pope ate in the great refeĉtory,[29] and at a separate
table were seated all alone the Count of Pallares and
Pero Niño. During the feſtival the Corsairs went
to sea.

> .   .   .

While matters were thus, Pero Niño fell ill. The
Pope's knights came to see him, and there likewise
came to him the moſt famous crossbowmen that were
in that country, Antonio Bonhora, Francisco del
Puerto, and other good men with the arbaleſt, drawn
thither by the fame of Pero Niño, to see and try his
arbaleſts. He had many good ones with him, and one
amongſt them, famous and ſtrong, which was called
La Niña. They tried this one, but could not bend it.
Then Pero Niño rose from his bed, although it was
the hour of his fever, and putting on a shirt, bent the
arbaleſt from the belt.

After he had purged away his illness he rose vigorous
and learned that the Corsairs' galleys had left, whereat
he was much displeased; but he hid his displeasure.

He took leave of the Pope and his knights, left Marseilles and set out in search of them. At nightfall, he came before the city of Toulon. There, there were ſtranded by the shore three sailing ships of the great Corsair Diego de Barrasa, who had run them aground when he found himself chased by a number of Genoese vessels and had abandoned them, leaping ashore with all his men. The captain got information and learned that the Corsairs whom he sought had crossed to Sardinia or to Corsica.

As soon as the captain had learned that the Corsairs had turned towards Sardinia, he held a council and declared that his will was to go and look for them. The sailors told him that the wind was already very ſtrong from the eaſt, and that eaſterly winds are violent in these latitudes ; that, moreover, it was getting on for dusk, when no ship should put out to sea when it was to enter the main, especially with a look of bad weather. But Pero Niño, who took no account of any danger when it was a queſtion of gaining honour, had so great a wish to catch these Corsairs, that he forgot all perils and toils which might befall. Againſt the wisdom of the sailors and in spite of the bad weather, he ordered the anchors to be weighed and the course to be set for the islands ; and he set out, like an eagle that goes to look for its prey when it desires food. However, when they left the shelter of the land, they found so ſtrong a gale blowing at sea that the galleys were in great difficulties and the sailors wished

65

to go back into the roads ; but the captain bade them busy themselves in making the beſt of it and not to speak more of turning back.   So the sailors commended themselves to God, shipped the oars, set the ſtorm trysails, fixed auxiliary rudders,[30] hoiſted the sails and put ſtrong and skilled men at the helms who could control them well.   The wind worsened as they went, and with the great force of the waves the auxiliary rudders of the captain's galley were unfixed,[31] and it was near sinking.   All called upon St Mary for succour, and then they recovered the rudders and brought in sail, and sent everyone below and faſtened the hatches of the *escandelar*[32] and of all the other cabins.   But the captain would never let himself be shut in, although it is the cuſtom, and the more because his cabin is by the prow of the galley where the waves wash aboard. On the contrary, he came out to see what was happening and told the sailors that he marvelled at their fear, for in a great wind there were waves as high as those on a river.   The gale increased every moment.   The sailors hoiſted the trysails a little way, tightened the sheets, fixed bunts to the sail, and ſtrengthened the tackle and the ſtop of the lateen yard, set two men to watch at each fall and bade them look out for squalls.[33] The wind blew on the prow : so all night the galleys hugged the wind.[34]   The force of the waves sprung the timbers and she shipped much water, so that the men at the prow[35] were busied all night in baling her ; moreover there was a heavy fog and it rained, which added to the sailors' toil.   All were at prayer, making vows to God and the saints for deliverance ; and they made the vow to make a pilgrimage to St Mary of

Guadalupe. And it pleased God that the wind should change a little towards the morning watch ; and the sea went down, and the wind veered to the north. Great was their joy ; each gave thanks to God for His deliverance. They hoiſted the lateen yards that before had been at half-maſt ; they loosened the tackle and the braces of the sail. At sunrise they sighted the Islands and at noon the galleys reached an island called La Capraja,[36] where there is a caſtle. There they caſt anchor. The inhabitants brought the captain an offering of bread and wine ; the crew ate, reſted and set all things in order again. When the meal was ended, they unshipped the oars, and the galleys went to search all the little islands where the Corsairs might have hidden themselves. They firſt visited La Gorgona,[37] then La Planosa, then searched all the harbours of the eſtuary of Bonifacio, which are in Corsica. There they only found a ship of Aragon. Thence they went to Sardinia, to Longosardo,[38] and Alguer.

In the Port of Alguer the captain found three Corsair ships, great and well manned, of which he had had no knowledge before he got there, and they did not know what they were. The men in the ships at once perceived the galleys, which they saw were of Caſtille, and forthwith set themselves to make ready for them. They warped themselves in by their anchors right under the walls of the town, for the sea washes the walls, and set up gangways from one ship to the other.

Alguer is a town of a thousand inhabitants, set in a plain, fortified with a good wall with strong towers. On the land side is a wide moat filled with water and men enter the city by a drawbridge. At this time the King of Aragon held in Sardinia only Longosardo, Alguer, and the castle of Cagliari ; all the rest of the country had rebelled against him. Those who were then masters in Sardinia were Micer Blanque, Judge of Arborea, and the lord of Monleone. The Corsairs were welcomed and well treated there for they brought provisions of all kinds to that country, and they helped them when they had need of it ; so that all the Corsairs who went there accounted themselves safe-guarded.

When the captain saw what they were, he ordered the King's standard to be hoisted and all his men to arm. Then he sent to summon them to surrender. Meanwhile, they had got close in under the city, whence reinforcements of men and arms crossed over to them. The captain who held the city on behalf of the King of Aragon came to the galleys and earnestly begged the captain on behalf of the King of Aragon to leave these Corsairs in peace, saying that they could not live without them, since it was only they who guarded the harbours, and brought them provisions ; he further invited him to land and enter Alguer, promising that he would make them render all service and honours.

The captain took counsel : that if he went ashore with the Corsairs, he might have to deal at the same time with them and with the people of the city who might unite against him ; and at all hazards he wished to board the ships. But the shipmaster and the overseers bore witness against this, that the galleys might well be lost in little time, if they had to fight not only against the ships but also against the people of the town ; and although he would not be beaten by these fears, he let himself be beaten by reason. When the matter was settled, the Corsairs thought that God had been very merciful to them. The captain went ashore and was received with great honour. He met the captain of the Corsairs ; but he would never speak with him and gave him to understand that he would rather have found him outside the Port. However, having learned from some of them that other Corsairs had carried off from merchants of Seville a sailing ship, well manned and richly laden, and had brought her to a harbour called Orestano, he went to that harbour and fought the ship, and took her quickly.

After he had taken the sailing ship the captain had news that the King of Tunis had manned certain galleys, and he went to look for them.

Our galleys set out towards Tunis and crept along the coast of Barbary, as secretly as they could. They drew near to the island which is called Zimbre ; it lies near another little island named Zimbrot.[39] Both are towards the Cape of Africa, five leagues from Tunis. Zimbrot is a desert island ; there are in it many springs of sweet water, much game and many birds that nest there. The galleys cast anchor there, and our men

refted there for several days, for they were much
wearied by the sea, hoping that some Moorish sailing
ship or carrack should pass; but none were seen. Thence
the land was clearly seen, and one night, in bright
moonlight, they left the island and fteered ftraight for
the Port of Tunis. For the ten days that the galleys
had been in that place, never had they lighted a fire,
and the captain, no more than his men, had eaten
boiled or roaft meats. And if they had ftayed there
longer, they would have had good fortune, for the
Moorish galleys were not long in coming thither.

The galleys rowed along very quietly, that neither
noise of oar striking water, nor any speech might be
heard, as muft be done by whosoever would make
his way into so fair a haven as is the harbour before
this city of Tunis, where lives one of the moft mighty
of all the Moorish kings, and where there are ever
sailing ships and light galleys lying manned. Thus
rowing and keeping watch on every side, about a league
before the entrance into the harbour, they sighted a
galley lying at anchor. The captain ordered that
they should make for her and grapple her. The
mafters of the oarsmen said: " My lord, if we lay our
grappling irons upon her, it may hap that other galleys
shall come upon us; and then we should wish to free
ourselves and we could not." The captain answered :
" At this hour I see no other in sight. Grapple with
her ; then when the others come, if it please God, we
shall have finished with this one."

Thereupon the trumpets sounded and they drew
near to the ship. The Moors had not seen the
captain's galleys until they were upon them:

nevertheless they defended themselves a good time. Finally, we took the galley, and killed or captured all the men we encountered. On the captain's galley there were men who spoke and underſtood the Arabic of this country. They learned from the prisoners that another galley lay ready manned within the harbour.

The prisoners, having confessed all they knew, and having told that there was yet another galley manned, very great (it was the great galeasse of the King of Tunis), our galleys began to enter the harbour, that they might seek it out. They would have surprised it like the other, but that there was in those parts a Genoese carrack, which by day anchored at the harbour mouth and left it at night. The Genoese had heard the noise of the fight at the taking of the firſt galley, and thinking that it was they that we were after, they ſtood to arms and sounded a trumpet. The Moors on the galeasse caught the sound; they weighed anchor and sighted the captain's galleys swooping down upon them, as bold as eagles that fall upon their prey. So soon as they saw us they bore away to the land and threaded their way into the channel of a river⁴⁰ which flows into the harbour. The captain's galley followed them, fighting its way by dint of pulling into this same channel, which was so narrow that perforce one galley had to go behind the other. At laſt, the captain's galley drew close in to their poop, and as they drew close he leapt across on to it.

71

But at the shock of striking his galley was thrown back and he found himself alone in the galley of the Moors.

The arms that he bore were these : a cuirass, vambraces, a steel cap, a sword and a targe ; and eagerly did he begin his battle against the Moors. The galley of Fernando Niño could not get near. In the captain's galley so great was the press to bear off the galeasse of the Moors, which had run aground, and to attack, and to defend themselves (for the Moorish galley was higher than ours) that men took no thought for the captain, for only those who were on the poop had seen him leap across. He cried out to them for help, but in so great a noise he was not heard. Every moment more men came up on the land side, where there were already many folk. They came into the sea to fight and their number grew so great that our men could no longer make any resistance.

The good knight, seeing that he would have no help unless it were from God and that he must go through with this undertaking to its end by himself, fought so lustily that it is a matter hard to believe except for those who saw him. He struck such good blows, killed and wounded so many, that in a short time he had fought himself free of them all and had driven them before him into the middle of the ship. There he laid hands on the Arraez of the galley (who is the Admiral) and having wounded him he made him stay stock still in one place, without daring to move.

Already day was breaking, and the Moors saw that all this havoc was wrought by one single man in their midst. They turned upon him like mad dogs and

ſtruck at him so hard that he could offer no resiſtance
and they bore him backwards almoſt to the poop.
The good knight, when he saw himself in such a pass,
called upon St Mary to help him and there made a
solemn vow. Then he hurled himself upon them,
fierce as a lion who throws himself upon his prey,
ſtriking, killing, driving them before him on to the
deck, which he swept clean up to the prow. Then his
own galley came up, and his men climbed into the
Moorish galley, and she remained in their hands;
but she was ſtill aground.

There, on the prow, he found himself face to face
with a Moorish knight, of whom he had much to tell
later, and he swore that this Moor ſtruck him so hard
on the head with his sword, that his knees bent beneath
the blow. Here did Pero Niño receive several great
wounds.

As soon as the day had dawned our men saw that
Moorish troops were muſtering near the city in such
a press that they covered all the ground as they passed.
None the less we went on labouring to get the great
galley off again, that we might carry her away with us.
We were near enough to land to touch it, and the
shore in this place is flat; the Moors came into the
water on their horses and fought with the men
in the captain's galleys. There were already more
than ten thousand Moors in the sea, of whom many
died therein. The conflict and the cries from one side
and another passed all description; so great was the
multitude that an arrow could not have been loosed
among them without finding a mark, nor a blow ſtruck
that did not ſtrike home.

Our men's desire to bear off the Moorish galley led them to forget the captain's galley, and she was all but loſt, for the Moors laid hands on her sides in such numbers that they dragged her to the shore. Seeing this, the captain leapt on to his galley with some of his folk; but it was a miracle that any man could yet save her from the hands of the Moors. So great a massacre was made there that the water round the galleys was all red with blood. While they fought, the Moors removed some of the timbers beneath the prow of their galley, and the water flowed in and filled her. When they saw the water coming in, they told the captain to labour no longer to take her, for it was no longer possible to bear her thence; and then they sacked her. Thereat the captain went back to his own galleys; but when they tried to row his own galley out they could not move her, for she had run aground at the prow. They asked his cousin's galley that was nearer the mouth of the channel to give them a tow, which she did. Thus rowing, they got themselves out of this pass.

When the fight was ended and the captain had recognised that he could not float the galeasse off, likewise that he could not carry off the other galley that he had taken, for he had not men enough and was far diſtant from any Chriſtian land, he caused everything to be removed that could be taken out of her, and then ordered them to set fire to her, and thus both were burnt. There was found therein fair booty of

74

crossbows and arms and other things which pertain to the armament of a war galley ; and on the galeasse they took two great banners of silk and gold, the faireſt in the world. Then the galleys drew off from the shore, and anchored, and they set about tending their wounded, of whom there were enough. The captain on that day received many blows from ſtones, lances and arrows. He was very weary and much bruised ; but what made him suffer moſt was a wound from an arrow that had gone through his leg, which galled him much ; but so long as the battle laſted he felt nothing. His men then ate and reſted : they had need.

While the galleys were anchored, there came to them in a rowing boat a Moorish knight sent by the King of Tunis to discover what men they were and to what country the galleys belonged. They told him that they were galleys of Caſtille. The Moor did not know what meant Caſtille. He asked if they were "Alfonsis". They told him Yes. (By that it muſt be underſtood that this name is ſtill used for Caſtillians in that country, since the time of the good kings who were named Alfonso, such as were Don Alfonso the Chaſte, and Don Alfonso the Catholic, and Don Alfonso the Great, and Don Alfonso, son of Don Pedro, lord of Cantabria,[41] and the Emperor Don Alfonso and Don Alfonso that gained the viſtory of Benamarin and others named Don Alfonso, all noble and saintly kings, who wrought great deſtruction among the Moors and won back the country where now we live, that before them had been loſt : by reason of the nobility of these kings were the Caſtillians called Alfonsis.)

75

When the Moor had learnt what they were, he went back to the King, and thence returned again and said to the captain that the King had sent him to ask wherefore he had wrought such havoc in his harbour; that if he had been warned in time, he would have given him better than he received; that there dwelt with this King men of our country to whom he shewed kindness and gave of his goods; and that he would do as much to our captain, if he would take what was offered him with a good grace; and that he besought him to do no more damage than had already been done.

The captain answered: " Say to the King that I thank him and give him grace for his good words, but that I do not go coursing up and down the seas to receive gifts in such wise of any man, but only to fulfil the orders of my lord, the King; howsoever, tell him that to do him pleasure I will shortly go hence, and that I have no intent to moleſt him more at this present."

. . .

The captain left Tunis, and the galleys, keeping close to the shore, passed before the cities of Bona and Bougie, near which there is a wood full of monkeys. As they encountered no more Moorish ships they left the coaſt and entered the gulf. At sea they found a galiot to which they gave chase. They overtook it; it was a ship of Aragon. On board were some Brothers of the Order of the Trinity, who were going over to Barbary to ransom captives. In the same manner they ſtopped several ships of Aragon and other Chriſtian countries, which coſt them no more pains than that of chasing them, thinking that they might be Moors,

and then they let them go in safety. After they had
thus beaten the seas for some days, seeking for hostile
ships and finding none, the captain returned to
Cartagena.

There he found his sailing ships, the one he had
taken from the Corsairs and the one he had manned
himself. This latter, on her way through the Straits,
had seized a rich Moorish caravel, in which they
captured Moors and stuffs of gold and silk, a quantity
of Arab cloaks,[43] dates, kegs of butter, corn, barley,
and many other things.

As soon as he reached Cartagena, the captain sent
to the King all the Moors that he and the others had
taken, and shared the rest of the booty with his men,
and satisfied them all. Then he landed the wounded,
and ordered them to be tended. They cleaned the
galleys, and the mariners replaced or repaired the
rigging, sails, oars and other matters, that they had
lost or damaged either in battle or in tempest. The
captain gave out crossbows to the crossbowmen who
had broken theirs, and furnished them with quarrells.
He completed the victualling of the galleys, with corn,
wine, bacon, cheese, water, wood and everything
needful, as at the beginning of his cruise. He was
resolved to go back once more to the coast of Barbary.
The surgeons told him to rest, not to take to sea again,
that his wound was serious, that it would become
worse with the weight of armour and the dampness
of the sea, that he was going to run great risks; but
they could never persuade him to stop. On the
contrary he bade everyone be ready on the appointed
day. His plan was made; he took with him the

galiot of Cartagena which he had manned as well as a galiot which had come thither from Aragon to offer its service to him, paid the crew of this laſt, withdrew all the men from the sailing ships, and had them come on the galleys, to bring them up to ſtrength.

The galleys set out from Cartagena. They reached the main and sailed along all day under their great sails and mizzensails.[44] As night fell the wind freshened from the eaſt. They lowered the great sails and mizzensails and hoiſted the ſtorm trysails. It blew very hard; in a short while they had made great way; already they could see the Barbary coaſt and the sharp rocks of Oran. Their counsel was to lower the sails and not to draw into the land, that they might not be discovered. The galleys remained in the open sea until night had fallen. When it was dark, they manned the sweeps and went to lie among the islands of Habiba.[45]

There is in these islands great quantity of birds who neſt there, cushats, sparrow-hawks, bitterns, sea-mews, falcons, quails,[46] and other birds of divers sorts, so many that the crews of all the galleys had as much as they could eat. These islands are desert; no man lives there, for no sweet water is found. Our men lay hid there, hoping that some Moorish vessel would pass by.

When the captain saw that none passed, he summoned the shipmaſters and the officers of the galleys to a council, and asked them if there were not on this coaſt

some place that they might put to the sack. The
master of the Aragon galley said that nearby was an
aduar that had about three hundred inhabitants and
that was about two miles from the sea. Thereupon
they agreed upon a plan. They waited until nightfall.
As soon as it had come, the galleys left Habiba and
drew near to the mainland, which was two miles off.
The captain ordered all his men to arm. He and they
landed ; he arrayed them, and told them what order
and what direction they were to keep ; how they were
to send two men forward who should get into the
village, learn the lie of the land and note all the
entries and egresses. He ordered that the standard
should wait at the entrance to the *aduar* with the
trumpets, and named those who should remain near it.
Then he chose those who should have the charge of
guarding the entries to the place, and who and how
many should go in to sack, and capture, and slay and
fire. He ordered that no man should heed to take
things which would encumber him, save only men,
women and children ; and that those whom they
could not capture and carry off should be put to the
sword and slain. As that which God has willed must
happen and cannot fail, even as the Prophet says :
" Man proposes, and God disposes " : so our men set
out and went their way.

Well would the captain have liked to go with them,
for he had never such confidence when he sent men out
as when he went with them : for men have ever better
heart and do more bravely when their lord is with them,
than when they set out without him. True that he
sent with them brave fellows, who knew well how to

command and to lead ; but when the bad soldier has
not to fear the eye of his captain, easily may he lose
all shame, and others may do likewise through fear.
Finally, although he had given them good leaders and
had committed the affair to them, he also sent with
them his cousin, Fernando Niño, for he himself was
suffering from the wound he had received at Tunis,
as I have declared before, and his leg could not bear
him. He remained on the shore with a few of his
men, and since he could do nothing more, he prayed
God to guide and guard his Chriftians.

When our men were gone some diftance from the
shore, they sent the two men forward, and awaited
their return a good two hours. They came back
saying that they had not been able to find the *aduar*.
Day was already beginning to break. Our men then
set out on the march again, letting those lead who had
some knowledge of the country, but they found neither
path nor village. Often did they hear the barking of
dogs, and bore off in that direction ; then they heard
nothing more and found nothing. They came among
tilled fields, but this only served to throw them into
disorder ; for they scattered, some going one way and
some another, saying that they would end by discover-
ing the village ; and they found nothing.

By now the sun shone on all the countryside.
Fernando Niño and Ruy Gutierrez de Bear, a good
gentleman who was there with some of his men,
rallied round the banner, and had all their men
recalled. They held that even if the village could be
seen and found, it was no longer the time to undertake
anything that had been planned ; for such work muft

be done at break of day, and altogether finished by
sunrise, since later the folk are all about abroad.
Moreover, our men were already in great jeopardy,
since they knew not whether they had been discovered,
and feared that they would soon be marked, since near by
there were several towns in which were many men
and horses, and it was already the hour of tierce, and
they were as much as a league and a half from the sea.
The ſtandard was borne back to the captain, and with
it came the men, all heavy at heart and full of shame.

When they came near to the sea they found the
captain on the shore, armed as he beſt might be, waiting
for them and full of care because they were so late.
But when he saw that they had nothing he was wroth
with those to whom he had given charge of the affair,
telling them that they were men of no counsel and
little action, and saying that if he had gone with them,
the matter would have turned out better than it had
done. He said: "That which angers me is not so
much the profit that you have loſt and the booty
that you have not brought back : it is the abasement
that you have all brought this day upon me and upon
my honour."

They boarded the galleys again. During the whole
day the captain remained invisible. In the third
watch he summoned the captains of the ships, the
maſters of the oarsmen and some few squires and
knights of those who were about him and said to them :
"Kinsmen and friends, well know ye how our lord
the King is noble and great-hearted ; how he has
chosen me and the reſt of you for this enterprise ;
how he has had these galleys manned better than were

ever galleys manned that left Castille before; and how, besides the great laying out of money ordered by him, he has bestowed many gifts and favours, to each according to his rank. Well should ye understand that so fair a usage has not been granted to me or to you for any other end than for us to return more for more, and that we are bound to do more than any man before us. Ye know well likewise how all our enterprises, up to this day, have been fair and honourable, since we left Seville. Now to begin well and not to bring to an end is no fair achievement, for it is in the ending that honour lies. Any man may begin a thing, but few can persevere to the end. If this time all has not gone well through some want of judgment, another time you shall do better. We are in the enemies' country; we shall have opportunity to make good our mistake."

When the captain had finished his admonishing, the shipmasters answered: "My lord, neither we nor the others have left undone anything that lay in our power. All night have we borne toil hard enough, clambering hills, dropping down into valleys, making our way through difficult country and enduring much labour; having regard to the hour of the day, it would have needed that God should work a miracle for us not to have been discovered, and, at the distance which we were from the sea, for us not to have all perished, like many others before us who have perished in this land."

When the discussion was ended and a council held, the captain ordered the galleys to keep along the coast and before daybreak they put men ashore to reconnoitre. They laid hands on a Moor, and queftioned him. He told them that the *aduar* they had searched for[47] was besieged by a Moorish Arab called Mahomed Muley Hadji, who had with him fifteen hundred horse ; and that he had left his *alhorma*[48] near a seaport called Arzeo-el-Belli : the women and children were there and all the heavy baggage.

The Arabs are a race of folk who always live in the open country. They take about with them their wives, their children and their flocks, and all the movables that they possess. They sow their corn and their other grain in one countryside, then leave it and go to another and do the same. When it is time they come back to harveft what they have sown. They have no land which is accounted theirs especially more than another. They are great gentlemen and are descended from those who were lords of Spain from the time King Rodriguez loft our land until the Kings of Leon drove them out, each in his own time, and after them the kings that were in Caftille. They go about always armed for war, and serve whom they will. When the realm is at peace, they seek adventures on their own account, cut the roads and capture those who pass. If they think themselves ftrong enough to attack a village, they surround it and let no man out to go to his work until they have paid ransom, as much as the place admits. They are very many, and spread over many countrysides.

But as it is written above : " He whom God guards is well guarded ", and as says the Chapter : " If God

be with us, no man is against us ", so God disposed
matters better than men had planned them. This
village which they had searched for to sack it, was
held in siege by the Arabs ; and it pleased God to
hide it from their eyes, so that they might not
all perish; for the unfaltering faith and devotion
which Pero Niño ever had towards God saved him
and his men, and because of his fidelity that he
had always kept he was saved from the hands of his
enemies.

Behold the great miracle which God wrought : the
hiding of the village from the eyes of his Christians,
so that they might not be utterly lost. Yet the
captain had brought with him a man born and bred
in that country, who had a wife and children at
Seville. There were also there men of Cartagena
and Aragon who had come to this coast in galleys
before. The country where they landed was known
to them ; often before had they seen this village
and several other *aduars* near it ; the landmarks
they encountered shewed them that they were near
it ; and they might well marvel that they could not
reach it.

At dawn the galleys reached an anchorage, where
there was a sandy shore which is called Arzeo-el-Belli.
The captain commanded that all his men should arm
themselves and go ashore and he disposed them as
was fitting. When it was fully light, they saw many
herds of cows and sheep in the country beyond. The

captain had his ſtandard and men at arms set on the rocks which edged the shore near the galleys and ordered the light-armed men,[49] crossbowmen and sailors, to surround all these cattle which went about in several herds, and to drive them towards the sea. In a little time they were all driven down ; they surrounded the beaſts on a part of the land from which they could not escape, and nimble men, armed with lances and swords, went into the midſt of them, to hamſtring them and slaughter them. Soon the shore was covered with slain beaſts so that it was piteous to see. They took what they liked and caſt the reſt into the sea. While this was being done, many Moors came up and the men from the galleys engaged in battle with them. The Moors took to flight, that they might draw our men away on to their fields. The Chriſtians so rushed out to pursue them that they were soon half a league from the shore, and though the trumpets sounded the retreat they were so far from the sea that they did not hear them. The captain then ordered that the men at arms should go forward with the ſtandard in support, for he feared leſt they should be close pressed by the Moors and not be able to make their way back.

When they reached the top of a hill looking over the plain they saw quite near in front of them the *alhorma* of the Moors, where there were many tents, for the moſt part black. There was there a ſtern fight, the Chriſtians fighting to take the tents and the Moors to defend them. The Moors divided into two bands. While one band fought, the others loaded their beaſts and their camels and took to flight with

the women and children from the other end of the
encampment. The Christians did not perceive this
until they had got into the tents. And it pleased God
that the Christians should be the victors; they went
into the tents, striking and killing the Moors around
them, and thus made themselves masters of the tents.
They found there a quantity of carpets, royal and
small *alcatifas* and *alfombras*,[50] worked in divers
manners; many casks and jars of butter and of honey;
salt and smoked meat; bread and corn; dates and
almonds, and dishes all prepared for those that had
time to eat them; ostrich feathers and packets of
porcupine quills. The light-armed men, crossbowmen and sailors, took as much of these things as they
could carry away and set fire to the tents. But while
they were coming back thus laden, the Moors had
gathered together again in greater number; they
surrounded the Christians on every side and bestirred
themselves to fall upon them. By reason of every
man's desire not to let go what he had carried off,
our men remained burdened with their spoil and could
not well fight. But the good men who were not
covetous of such things, but only of doing what must
be done at such times, forced the others to lay down
their booty, reproaching them and encouraging them
and shewing them the danger in which they stood.
It is certain that great covetousness blinds a man and
prevents him from doing what he should, and often
causes him to lose that which he should hold most
precious. Therefore the good soldiers made them
cast away their booty, saying that every man must
fight hard to save his own life: and they bade all

take heed not to run towards the sea, for no man could so make his escape, since every moment Moors came up on horseback and the way was long. The booty was then set down on the ground. Our men betook themselves to fighting bravely, ſtriking the Moors to such purpose that they drove them back, and slew many among them, of whom, as it appeared, was one ſtruck and slain who seemed to be a great man among them; for all the Moors gathered round him and bore him away down a valley making great lamentation over him. While they were thus gone with their Moor, the Chriſtians took up their booty again and set out on the march once more united; and soon the galleys came into view. Imagine what the good knight felt, when he did not see his men; and then when he saw them again and could not come to their help. Our men made ſtraight for the galleys, but already the Moors shewed themselves in greater multitude than before.

In this place there was a clump of evergreen oaks, which might afford shelter. They agreed that the men at arms and the crossbowmen should do battle with the Moors and offer a front to them, retreating from time to time when they could, so as to give those who carried the booty time to get away. Thus fighting and retreating they got near the galleys. Pero Niño then came to their help, when they were already hard pressed by the multitude of Moors drawn up before them; and it was not long before the horsemen came up who had been busied before Arzeo-el-Belli.

Near the galleys there were some rocks. As the

spot was well known, and Muley-Hadji, chieftain of
all this tribe and brother of the King of Benamarin,
had come up with his men, Pero Niño commanded
that the ſtandard should not be withdrawn all day,
but that the men at arms and a few crossbowmen,
with shield-bearers, should make a ſtand round it and
fight to defend the rocks. While some defended the
rocks, the reſt went to eat, and when these came back,
the fighters had their turn. So passed the whole of a
day, so full of hardship and peril that no man who was
there will ever to my belief see the like. Many times
did the Moors almoſt force an entry on to the rocks ;
and then again the Chriſtians would capture the land
they held ; then the Moors came back, angry as lions,
and drove the Chriſtians so far that some would be
caſt into the sea. Once it befell that as they
skirmished, some of our men advanced too far and were
about to be taken. To come to their aid the Chriſtians
attacked in mass, leaving the rocks. Then the Moors
all threw themselves upon them, and it went ill with
the Chriſtians, for already they were cut off from the
sea. When Pero Niño saw his men in such jeopardy,
he leapt ashore, and made all the others who remained
land with him down to the laſt. The galleys were
left in the keeping of God, and the captain went to
the help of his men. There was there a great fight,
for every Moor in the country had come up, and, if
the captain had not landed, his men would all have
been loſt. But it pleased God that this time the Moors
should be beaten, for the crossbows wrought such
havoc in their midſt, and in the end they drew off from
the sea againſt their will, leaving many dead and

prisoners. The captain then withdrew his ſtandard and all his men.

Although he had come so well out of this affair, the captain was ſtill none too content, for he had not succeeded in putting any town of this country to the sack. They bore away to the open sea, so long as daylight laſted, so that the Moors should see the galleys going away, and should think that they were returning to Chriſtian lands; but when night had fallen the galleys turned and made again for the Barbary shore. The captain had good pilots who knew that coaſt, and during the night they visited all the coves, creeks and anchorages which are in these parts; and after the hour of tierce the galleys sought shelter in a creek. As soon as it was day our men set look-outs ashore on a high place which could be seen from the sea, and from which all the country lay revealed: they were to make known by signals what they saw. At the same time they sent a few men into the fields to reconnoitre, if they could, who came to an *aduar* of four or five houses, but they found there neither man nor woman. They took all they could carry off of clothes and valuables and got back without having been seen. They said that they had seen further off many people reaping and working in the fields and that it was not a place on which to make a descent, as it was full of people. In the meanwhile, the Moors had discovered the look-out, and coming nearer they saw the galleys. Soon after, columns of smoke arose up all over the country, and multitudes of people ran up. Those rocks, where the captain had taken up a position, were antimony mines.

The galleys set out once more, making their way along close to the coast. Many Moors had already reached the shore, and the galleys, as they went, covered them with arrows. The captain followed in a long-boat protected with shields,[51] with two crossbow-men, who bent strong arbalests for him, and he made fair shots, well aimed, striking men and horses. Night fell as the galleys arrived before the town of Oran. During the most part of the night, the galleys did not cease from firing bolts and quarrells dipped in tar into the town, which is near the sea. The noise and the cries which came from the town were very great by reason of the havoc that was wrought.

On the morrow, the galleys were before a little fortified town that is called Mazalquebir, that they might capture a great galley which should have been lying under its walls, but already she had been hauled ashore. A good part of the day passed in attacking the town with bolts and quarrells, and then the galleys went and cast anchor before the caves of Alcocevar. There they passed the night. The captain held a council with the mariners and shipmasters. They said they had no more fresh water and that they must find some, but that in this place it would be a dangerous matter. " The galleys ", said they, " have been sighted from the land ; the people of the country are all warned and afoot ; already they guard the watering places. But if we make for the main, we have very little water ; it may hap that a contrary wind should

arise before which we should have to run, and the
want of water would hinder us." The captain
answered : " Friends, whatsoever is certain and forced
upon us needs no counsel. In a certainty there lies
more peril than in a matter of doubt. The certainty
is that we have no more water, and without water we
cannot live. Make for the land and let us go ashore.
While some fight, let the others get water."

In this place there is beside the sea a peak of rock,
and at the foot of the rock, looking seawards, are caves
that could hold many men, and within them abundance
of fresh water is to be found. To reach the top of the
rocks is a rough climb. The Moors held the plateau
in great numbers and the galleys were so close in shore
that ſtones hurled by the Moors fell on board, from which
in turn many were hurled againſt them. The crossbowmen of the galleys for their part killed and wounded
many. They bent mighty crossbows for the captain,
with which he aimed moſt signal shots, ſtriking both
men and horses. But however many fell, there was
such a multitude of Moors that they never seemed any
the fewer for it ; and they would not leave the plateau,
so that they harried our men, who were getting water,
with their ſtones.

Then the captain gave orders that all the armed men
should land and should go to take the rocks from the
rear. He said to them: " Friends, you see in what ſtraits
we are if we get not our water. Go againſt them.
It is evident to you that I cannot go with you" (for he
was crippled from the wound he had received at
Tunis) ; " do ye as befits good men." Then they
landed and arranged themselves in very good order,

crossbowmen and shieldbearers. The Moors, when
they saw them, left the plateau of the caves, and went
for them like mad dogs, without any fear, and let fly
at them a hail of ſtones and came near enough to attack
with their lances. The Chriſtians remained very firm,
for such was their duty. This time they killed a good
number and the crossbows ſtruck down so many that
at laſt they drove them back. The captain, none the
less, made them take the water in great haſte and shoot
arrows at those who were above the rocks, so that they
were able to take all the water they needed. Then
they recalled all the men who were on shore, who
retreated with great peril and labour. Of those who
had set out from the galleys there were few who came
back without wounds, and even of those on board
some were hit.

The Moors had made there, on the banks of a
ſtream, a great ambuscade, but the men they had set
there neither left it nor showed themselves, hoping
that all our men would land, as they had done at other
times ; and when they saw only a few men and no
ſtandard, they did not reveal themselves. The captain
and our men guessed their reason well enough, for the
Moors from time to time took flight before them, so as
to draw them on in pursuit. When they had got the
water, the galleys drew off from the land. At once
the whole countryside was covered with people in such
multitude that no man could have made count of
them. Along the banks of a ſtream, where there were
many trees, they saw men on horseback. The captain
ordered them to shoot their bolts upon these banks,
and the ſtones fell in their midſt, and then they were

seen to go up the brook in great haſte. There may
have been five thousand horsemen ; the men on foot
were innumerable.

The galleys caſt anchor ; and then the men busied
themselves in eating and in tending the wounded. While
they were yet eating, the eaſt wind,[52] which is very
fierce in those seas, began to blow and became very
ſtrong, raising high and very violent seas. The galleys
haſtened to weigh anchor and by dint of heavy rowing
againſt the wind reached the Habibas Islands. There
they anchored until the wind should have dropped
enough to let them return to Spain. But each day it blew
harder, and the gale increased as one might expeſt at
that season, for already it was the month of Oſtober.
The captain resolved to try to get to Spain while his
provision of water laſted. They got out into the open
sea to set their course ; but they found the wind so
ſtrong and the seas so heavy that the galleys were
nearly engulfed and returned with great difficulty to
the islands they had left. Several times they attempted
to set out again to sea ; but each time the ſtorm drove
them back. They remained there fifteen days and
ſtill the weather grew no better. The captain and
his sailors agreed that they were in great jeopardy in
this desert island and that the crews muſt be rationed,
receiving bread by weight, water and wine by measure,
juſt as much as was needful if they were not to die of
hunger and thirſt. All, from the greateſt to the leaſt,
were set under this rule and even the captain obeyed it.
That was how he used to aſt, and that is always the
duty of him who has the leadership of a great company
and loves well his men ; in everything he should be

the first. Our Saviour, Jesus Christ has well said :
" I give you the ensample ; as I do, do ye also." It
is a truth, and every day it may be seen, that those
who are going into battle have a better purpose of
well-doing when the captain marches with them and
especially when he marches at the head, than when he
stays in the rear or goes not with them at all. Thus
the captain only drank one very little cup of water and
another of wine at his dinner and the same at supper.
During all this time he made them dig a well in the
island, thinking to find fresh water ; but the deeper
the well the dryer was the soil. Others before him
had dug in this place with the same intent and found
no more water than he did. Nevertheless, God, who
abandons not His own, provided for our men's needs
in some part. They were given barely enough bread
to sustain them ; but they found something to eat
by catching the birds who nest in very great number
on the soil of those islands.

Thus twenty days passed and the water was all
drunk. At last it pleased God that one night, towards
the morning watch, the sea went down and the wind
blew less hard. The captain summoned the sailors :
he told them that it would be well to try if they could
get water on the coast of Barbary and to run any risks,
as they were in such straits. When they had
deliberated, the galleys set out for a watering place
that is called El Bergelete.[53] It is on a coast where
dwell many folk, where great numbers of Moors are
wont to assemble ; and it is a most dangerous place,
where great troops may be hidden, for the country is
covered with trees and cut up by ravines. The

sailors bade the captain to consider well his intent; that the place was full of peril and the more as the sea was still rough; and several added that it would be a hard task to get water there: that once, men belonging to five Aragonese galleys had been massacred there; that many others had there perished; and indeed, that this place was nothing but a grave-yard for Christians. The captain answered: "Do you give me your warrant for matters that pertain to the sea; on land, God, who is ever wont to come to our help, will help us yet again and see that we do not perish. He who has struck water from the hard rock that all the people of Israel might slake their thirst, will easily bestow as much on us here and now if we have firm faith in Him. Let us pray Him to succour us in such a strait." Then he caused all his men to arm, and ordered that light armed and nimble men should go forward to see whether there were ambushes, and that in the event of their meeting no one, they should post look-outs on the highest point near the sea and make signals. Soon the look-outs signalled safety. The men at arms then landed and went right into the middle of El Bergelete. The galleys in the meantime took in as much water as they needed, until their butts and casks were full. That done, they called in the look-outs, and everyone went aboard safe and sound, giving thanks to God and to the Virgin Mary, whose help had never failed them. The anchors were not yet weighed when they saw the Moors come up in great numbers, searching for the Christians where they had passed, with drawn *gumias*: where they discovered their traces they struck, so that twenty or thirty of them came to slash the bushes where they saw the traces of a Chriſtian. So they came to the sea and hurled ſtones at the galleys ; but more than one remained sorely wounded or killed by the arbaleſts. Then the galleys made their way back, ſtriving with all their might againſt the sea, which was yet very ſtrong, to the Habibas Islands, where they had as it were, taken up their abode.

That night the captain summoned his sailors who were experienced in sea matters to a council. There came thither Micer Nicolaso Bonel, ship's captain of the captain's galley, a ſtrong knight and good mariner, who had often been at sea on great affairs and had been captain of galleys : Juan Bueno, who all his life had been going about in carracks, sailing ships and galleys, a proved mariner whose advice in sea councils was always surer than that of other mariners, and others, both maſters of oarsmen and mariners, ſtrong in body and skilled in their calling. Each gave his opinion. Some said that they could not help being carried away by the wind and that they muſt run before it.[54] With it blowing from the eaſt with such force it would soon blow them to Sicily. Others said that they could not hope to make Sicily, but muſt go to Rhodes ; and the others answered that it would be a long and perilous course and that they ought to try to make the Genoese or the Roman shore or else the Archipelago, where there are rich islands, full of many people and towns and cities, such as Candia, and Pera, and Modon and many others. None of the sailors was confident that they could run for Spain. The captain asked Juan his opinion of what ought to be done.

He answered : " My lord, when it is a queſtion of what God would do, no man can know it beforehand, since between night and morning God sends His grace to whomsoever it pleases Him. This night I could not give you an opinion which would be sound ; but to-morrow morning, if it please God, I will give the advice that seems good to me. In the meanwhile, be all ready to set out to sea."

That night, the moon shewed herself round as a ship, the points to heaven, the keel towards the sea. She was four days paſt the firſt quarter. In the firſt night watch, the wind calmed a little ; in the second watch, it began to blow from the south-weſt until morning. The sun rose brilliantly from the rocks. The sky was clear. All waited for the opinion of Juan Bueno, who was on the other galley, and all looked about them. Juan Bueno climbed into the waiſt of the ship with his face turned towards Spain ; he opened his arms and then began to make great geſtures ; for it was his cuſtom to speak but very little. The captain ordered that they should ask what meant these signs, and he replied that they should tell the captain to bid them set their course for Spain. The others would have prevented him, but it pleased the captain to follow his advice.

The galleys left Alhabiba and found the sea very heavy, and the wind blew from the weſt, very fresh. The sailors at once made ready. They set up their compasses furnished with magnet ſtones,[55] they opened their charts and began to prick and measure with the compass, for the course was long and the weather adverse. They observed the hour glass and entruſted it to a watchful man. They hoisted the storm try-sails, fixed the auxiliary rudders and shipped the oars. They began their voyage by calling upon the name of God. All day they sailed, having the wind and the seas on their cheek.[56] The waves came at them, and covered the galleys up to the middle of the decks. Thus they sailed along all day. At sunset, the moon appeared; little by little she ate up all the clouds, cleared the sky and shone brilliantly. The wind veered to the south. Thus they voyaged all night in great anxiety. At dawn they sighted the land of Spain. The seas were very heavy and by great force and toil the galleys reached a watering place called San Pedro de Arraez, which is on the coast of Granada. The crews rested there all day, and at night the galleys lay before Las Aguilas. The next morning they entered into the Port of Cartagena. The townsfolk were overjoyed and rejoiced much at the return of the captain, for he was beloved in that country. There all reposed themselves, lived on land, and refreshed themselves after their toil, of which they had had to bear enough. The captain paid off and satisfied the galleys of Aragon and of Cartagena.

Thereupon there came a letter from the King which bade him go with his galleys to Seville, leave them there and come to see him without delay. Then the captain had all the Moorish captives, and the other goods that belonged to the King, put on board to take them to the arsenal at Seville. The galleys set out; and on their course they stopped an Aragonese galiot which had been chartered by Barbary merchants. On this galiot there were Moors, negresses and other slaves ; and it was fully laden with wax, cochineal, cloaks and other merchandise of great price. The captain took all the merchandise and the slaves and let the ship go, as was equitable. Coaſting along the kingdom of Granada, the galleys passed through the ſtraits of Gibraltar and reached Cadiz.

The captain already felt very ill by reason of the wound that he had received in the leg before Tunis, and he went ashore. As soon as they arrived the wind had begun to blow so ſtrongly from the eaſt, that for a whole month not a single ship could either enter the Port of Cadiz or leave it. During all this time the captain sojourned there, without its being possible for him to depart. From this delay and from the lack of good surgeons it came about that the wound became very serious. At laſt the wind fell. Thereupon the captain left Cadiz and went up to Seville, where he was warmly welcomed by as many brave men as there were in the city.

The beſt surgeons of Seville met to examine the captain's wound. They found it so serious that several desired to cut off the foot, for there was danger of death ; and if the foot were cut off, there was a chance of life. The surgeons decided to tell him this, and he answered them : " If the hour when I muſt die is come, let it befall me as God wills. But for a knight it is better to die with all his limbs whole and united as God has given them to him, than to live wretched and crippled, and to look at himself and see that he is good for nothing." And he said further that they might arrange to perform any other operations that they would, but that as to cutting off his foot, he would never agree. The surgeons decided to cauterize the wound with a burning iron, and they told him that since matters were thus, he muſt bear this operation, and they would see if it would heal him.

They heated an iron, big as a quarrell, white hot. The surgeon feared to apply it and had pity for the pain it would cause. But Pero Niño, who was already used to such work, took the glowing iron in his hand and himself moved it all over his leg, from one end of the wound to the other. Without ſtopping, they gave him a second like it, and he applied it for the second time. He was not seen during all this time to give a single sign of pain ; no one heard him make any complaint. Thenceforward his wound was well dressed, and it pleased God that each day it should mend.

The captain ordered his galleys to be laid up, and went to find the King, who was then at Segovia. The King and all the knights at the Court gave him great welcome.

. . .

[1405] At the time of the rejoicings that the King made for the birth of his son, there came to the Court Ambassadors from France, whom King Charles had sent to the King Don Enrique, to ask him, according to the treaties and brotherhood that exiſted between them, for the help of galleys, sailing ships and soldiers. The King resolved to send them, and forthwith ordered the fleet at Seville to be manned. But as the galleys of Seville could come but late by reason of the diſtance, he had three galleys quickly manned at Santander, and set them under the orders of Pero Niño. Moreover, he had had sailing ships manned, and gave them for captain Martin Ruiz de Abendaño, and commanded him to set out as soon as he might with Pero Niño. The King further bade Pero Niño and Martin Ruiz wait for each other, and bear each other good company, although sailing ships and galleys can rarely keep together, since each night the galleys make for the land, whereas the sailing ships keep to the main, unless it be agreed that each shall await the other in the same harbour. The King had all things needful given to Pero Niño most nobly and according to his wont : arms, arbalests, and many coined crowns. He even gave him crossbowmen of his own household to go on board the galleys.

Pero Niño left the Court, and all his gentlemen trained to war with him, and went to Santander. There he found the galleys manned by good sailors and oarsmen, the best that they had been able to get together. He had landsmen brought to him and chose the best crossbowmen he could engage and good men at arms, fit to bear him aid in the affair he was charged with. He paid all his folk well and appointed the ship-captains of his galleys. He gave one to Fernando Niño, his cousin, the other to Gonzalo Gutierrez de la Calleja, a good gentleman of those parts, for Pero Niño was a great lord bred in that country in the right of his mother, who was of the house of La Vega.

Pero Niño left Santander with his galleys, keeping close to the coast on the look out for the sailing ships

of Castille. He went to Laredo, to Castro and to
San Vicente; but the ships were still at Santoña.
The galleys arrived at El Pasage, where is the frontier
between Gascony and Castille, and remained there
until a land wind arose good for crossing the sea of
Spain[57] and for going straight to La Rochelle. The
wind blew from the north east and the galleys reached
the open seas. The great sails and mizzen sails were
hoisted, and they sailed along all day out in the open
sea, steering towards the west. When night came,
the wind fell; they furled the sails and took to the
oars. Thus they went until the second watch; then
the wind flew round to the west, striking the galleys
on the cheek; then it blew harder from the south
west. They did not dare hoist sail, for fear of striking
the Maransin;[58] but instead they rowed with the wind
ahead to get away from the shore. Towards the
morning watch the wind dropped. They continued
to go towards the south west, and when day broke
they could no longer see either France or Spain.
Opinion was divided; in the end, as the moon was in
her first quarter and the wind from the west might
have become strong enough to cast the galleys on the
shore of the Maransin, it was decided that they must
go on rowing to get clear into the open sea. They
went all that day without knowing in what latitudes
they were. When they heaved the lead, they touched
bottom in sixty fathoms,[59] and knew that they were
near land, because the lead brought up sand, although
it was a rocky bottom. Seeing that they had been
drawn towards the coast, they agreed to try to
gain the open sea. For five days they sailed thus

without daring to approach the land. Then they made a calculation, according to the length of time they had sailed on that course, that they must be beyond all these perils,[60] and that if a strong breeze from the north arose, they could make neither France nor England. The galleys therefore steered for the north, sailing along day and night with much toil and peril. At the end of three days they sighted the coast of France and from dawn until the hour of vespers rowed hard and crowded on sail. The galleys drew near to the island of Ré, which is an island abounding in victuals, in cows, sheep, bread, wine and fruit; as many as three thousand men ready to bear arms dwell there. Above the Port is a monastery of the order of St Benedict. This island and the others dependent on it belong to France. There was the captain very well received. Thence the galleys went to La Rochelle, a city of France, very rich and always diligently kept on a footing of war. The captain was well received there, and they rendered him many honours. Much did they rejoice at his coming. There came to see him the High Constable Messire Charles de Lebret and many other personages who were there to guard the country. At that time began the war between France and England on account of the Duchy of Guienne, and because the English had slain their king, King Richard, who had married a daughter of King Charles of France.

.   .   .

The English are folk very diverse in character and different from all other nations. They are such for several reasons; the first is that they inherit it from those

whose descendants they are ; the other is because they
live in a country abounding in meat and victuals and
rich in metals ; and yet another cause of this difference
is that they are many in number in a little land. Even
though this land be great, I call it little in regard to
the number of people who live therein. They
maintain that there is never in this country a great
mortality or a bad year ; moreover, they are surrounded
by the sea and for this reason they have no fear of any
other nation.

.   .   .

King Richard of England wedded the daughter of
King Charles of France, and in the treaty of marriage
it was stipulated that the King of England should
renounce the claims he had in France, both in
Normandy and in Guienne ; and a perpetual peace
was sworn between them. When the English knew of
this peace, they were for the most part ill-content,
for they have no wish to live in peace with any other
nation, for peace suits them not, seeing that they are
so numerous that they cannot keep within their
country and in time of peace many cannot find
subsistence there. And if their king concludes a peace
with other countries, which forces him to give safe-
conducts to merchant vessels, very rarely do they
respect them. They have a liking for no other nation,
and if it happen that some valiant knight visits them,
as do often certain knights and gentlemen who travel
through divers parts of the world, whether to seek a
livelihood with a brave heart, or for feats of arms, or
for curiosity, or as ambassadors, the English try to
seek some way of dishonouring them or of offering

them an affront. Accordingly as I have said, they are very different from all the other nations.

. . .

[1405] The King Don Enrique sent to this war, and in support of the King of France, as has been told above, Pero Niño, captain of three galleys, and Martin Ruiz de Avendaño, with forty armed ships. Pero Niño, being at La Rochelle waiting for the Castillian fleet to start for England, resolved together with certain knights of France who were there, to enter the river of the Gironde, which was quite near, and to go as far as Bordeaux to try to capture some English vessels. The captain therefore set out with his galleys from La Rochelle, crossed the Pas-des-ânes,[61] entered the Gironde and went to Royan and Talmont,[62] two French towns which are on the bank on the side towards La Rochelle, and are always kept on a war footing; and there he was very well received by the knights who were in garrison there. Some came aboard his ships and there went with him two very light long-boats, which carried the French crossbow-men and archers. So that they might not be seen by the English, the galleys left Talmont in the second night watch, rowing with the tide. At dawn Bordeaux appeared. None being on their guard there, our men landed and pillaged several houses on the banks of the river. They took several prisoners and carried off cattle, cows, and sheep, and kept what they needed; then, coming again on board the galleys, they came before the city. Many sailing ships and other vessels were there; and when these saw the galleys, they spread sail, thinking that the galleys

would come up the river above the town ; but this
was not to be done, for the banks approached each
other, and arrows and darts reached the galleys from
both shores. Furthermore, the ships could have taken
the galleys from behind, coming up with the wind and
tide, so that the galleys could not do all that they
might have wished. Nevertheless, some have maintained that if the galleys had not ſtopped to plunder,
and had made ſtraight for the ships, they might have
taken them all, for they were not ready to fight,
having no knowledge of the galleys' coming: but once
they had been seen, the blow could not in any wise
be attempted.

.　　.　　.

More than a hundred boats and cutters manned by
men at arms came out from among the ships, and shot
so many arrows and bolts at the galleys that those
therein had enough to do to fight and defend themselves. There were four caſtles on the city side and
very near it, and the captain ordered men to go to
burn them. Then many men on foot and mounted
came out in arms from the city to defend these caſtles ;
but they could not get there soon enough to prevent
them from being all burnt. The galleys reached the
other side of the shore and the captain ordered all the
houses and all the corn (of which there was much in
this part) to be fired, and whosoever they found there
to be killed and plundered ; so that in a few hours
more than a hundred and fifty houses were in flames.
The captain would have liked to remain some days
in the Gironde to wreak more harm on the English
lands ; but he had news that the English fleet was then

PLATE III

[*Photo. Catala*

THE BURNING OF THE CASTLE

*From a miniature of the French translation of Livy. Paris, Bibliothèque de l'Arsenal,
MS. 5082, fol. 16*

[*face p. 106*

expected, and his plan was to get out of the river and to leave that country. That night the galleys returned to Talmont and did not cease from rowing all night, for a strong breeze had arisen coming from the bar, taking the galleys on the prow, and this wind might have brought up the English fleet. At dawn, when the galleys sought to cross the shoal, the tide began to make, so that the galleys were hard pressed to sail against wind and tide : and further the breeze had become very fresh and blew up the waves, so that all their stubborness was needed to reach the open sea. The mouth of the river is so wide here that it is more than a league from one bank to the other. They continued to fight thus against the wind and the current for a good two hours without making much headway. One galley would have gone aground if God had not willed to save her, and it was a great miracle that she was brought back, so far had she gone adrift. If the English fleet had appeared at that moment, the galleys would have been in great danger ; but it pleased God that they should cross the bar ; they entered the open sea and went back to La Rochelle. All those who had understanding in such matters marvelled at the great boldness and courage that the captain had shewn in penetrating to such a place, which other galleys had never reached, and in setting fire to the best guarded and most populous part of all Gascony.

While Pero Niño was at La Rochelle, there came thither, with two galleys, a French knight called Messire Charles de Savoisy.[63] He was a noble knight, an officer of the household of the King of France.

For some of those matters which may befall knights of great estate, he had been banished from the Court for two years. This lord was brave, enterprising, courteous, well equipped and rich. Some said he was in love with a great lady, and he certainly appeared to be, and gave it to be understood by his badges. He had come to Marseilles and had there had built at his own expense two good galleys, which he had fully manned with gentlemen and picked crossbowmen; and they were the best furnished and fairest galleys ever seen in our time. Well do I believe that the banners alone were worth as much as the fittings of an ordinary galley. Messire Charles had already had news of Pero Niño, who for his part had also heard tell of Messire Charles. They met, and had great pleasure in each other's company. Chance had well arranged things in thus bringing them together; for the qualities that each valued were found abundantly in the other. They agreed to sail together, to bear each other good company and not to leave each other during this war. They were likewise both resolved to go to England and to make first for the islands of Ouessant.[64] But Messire Charles and his mariners then said that there would be great danger in making for the cape of Ouessant, for they might strike the English fleet on the high seas; and that if the weather became bad, they would be in great danger from them; that, if the captain thought it good, it would be better to coast along Brittany, and that then they would not have so long a crossing. This pleased the captain, and the more since he knew that the Castillian ships were already off the Brittany coast. As for Messire Charles, he was so courteous a knight that it ever pleased him to recognise Pero Niño as captain ; and he asked him to light the lantern on the poop of his galley, according to the custom of a captain at sea, assuring him that he would follow him even as his own galleys did.

They set out from La Rochelle, passed before Les Sables d'Olonne and the mouths of the Loire, and touched at the town of Guérande.[65] Between Brittany and the islands there are the islands of Ré and Belle-Isle. Those who live in this last bear no arms and do not defend themselves, even when men seek to do them harm, because the Pope has taken them under his protection and excommunicates any man who attempts to harm them.

.   .   .

Thus sailing from port to port along the coasts of Brittany, they rounded the Cape of St Matthew[66] and entered the Race, which is twenty miles long. This Race is very dangerous. A man would think that the sea was boiling there in great bubbles, like water in a cauldron over the fire ; not, however, that it is hot, but the sea there is such that it is all whirlpools. In heavy weather the peril there is extreme and the ship that is dragged towards the coast is sunk in an instant. Neither oars nor sails serve there ; there must be good auxiliary rudders, for the currents are so strong and bear so hard upon the ship that, when God guards her from reefs, she may do these twenty leagues in three or four hours, and when the Race is passed, the sailors give thanks to God, Who has saved them. There the Flanders channel[67] begins, which continues up to the watch tower[68] in Flanders. After they had passed the Race, the galleys came to a port of Brittany and passed the night there. The next day they left there and passed through the Race of Blanchart.[69] This is not so long as the Race of St Matthew. On the morrow they passed through another, which is called the Race of St Malo. Thus sailing each day they reached the Port of Brest, which is a town of Brittany. There they met the fleet of Castille of which Martin Ruiz de Avendaño was captain. Pero Niño and Messire Charles spoke of the voyage to England with the captain of the ships, but they could come to no agreement with him, for, as was clearly manifest thereafter, he and his company wished to do nothing but make a profit with the merchants that they had brought.

.   .   .

When Pero Niño and Messire Charles saw that the captain of the ships was not willing to help them and to fight, they resolved between themselves to cross the sea and pass over to England.

That very night the sailors made everything seaworthy. They observed the sky and the signs were favourable : the sunset was clear and the moon was five days old ; she had one of her horns turned towards the sea. The galleys left the port at nightfall. During the whole of the first watch they rowed out into the open sea, their lantern lit on the stern of the captain's galley, and lay to on a grapnel[70] until the dawn watch to let the men rest. Then they set their course

weſt-north-weſt, the wind blowing from the weſt on the
galley's cheek; they hoiſted sail and the weather was
good. When day broke the wind dropped; they
unshipped the oars and rowed all day until evening;
then the wind freshened and became contrary, blowing
on the prow; they hoiſted ſtorm trysails and fixed
the auxiliary rudders. The weather promised ill.
The ship's captain[71] looked on every side, pale, sighing,
consulting compass and chart; he spoke low with the
sailors, and these had already beſtirred themselves to
work the vessel. The captain watched them and saw
in all this signs of a tempeſt. He summoned the sailors
to a council and asked them what these changes
signified; the pilot said to him: "My lord, leave all
cares to us others who have to do the work: it will serve
no purpose of yours to learn them." But the captain
insiſted, saying that he wished to know; and they
answered that a great ſtorm was gathering. "The
moon is new and already well on in her quarter: the
wind is veering to the weſt-north-weſt[72] and blows on
our prow, so that we cannot get to England. On this
course, if we return to France we shall be across the
Race: if we ſteer to the weſt, we can find no harbour.
If the wind ſtill freshens we muſt make once more
for Spain. The passage is long and dangerous, and
furthermore, we may meet the English fleet on our
way. There is then danger on every side, so we ought
to make ready in time." The captain ordered the
signal to be made to Messire Charles and to the
captains of the other galleys to come near his ship for
a council. They were asked what they thought of the
weather and of the look of things. Their conclusion

was to continue the voyage as they had begun it, to
try with all their might to get near the coast of
England, and, if they could not achieve it, to turn,
but for them all to follow the guiding lantern as long
as they could. This resolution taken, the wind
freshened, and blew so hard and so fierce and raised
such a sea, that the waves came aboard over the prow
up to the middle of the galleys and forced them round.
The waves were mountain high and the sea all hollowed.
The galleys were separated, each pursuing its course,
so that there were no longer any two together. In a
few hours they were all scattered, and lost to view,
so that none of them had any sight of the others and
they were several days without meeting. All this
night the captain's galley hugged the wind, until the
gale mastered it and then they had to run before it
and send all the crew below decks and batten down all
the hatches. There was no sail hoisted higher than
the height of a man. The waves were so strong that
as they struck the ship's quarter they threatened to
break her and made her sides ring again. And such
high seas came over the poop that some came right
into the galley. Such waves are the most dangerous;
they carried off the long boat from the place where
she was lashed and cast her into the sea. All the crew
despaired of their lives and prayed God to have pity
on their souls. So passed the whole night in a great
gale ; and moreover it rained, which is a thing which
is very troublesome to sailors. When dawn came one
of the galleys appeared, but so far off that they could
only see her sail against the main. The moon then
went into her first quarter, and it happened that

several times she disappeared and one would have said that she was swallowed up ; this disappearance was wrought by the height of the waves. Land was still not in sight on any quarter. Nevertheless continuing to head for France, at midday they sighted the spires[73] of the churches of France ; for in this part the coast of France is flat and low and affords no bearings. It pleased God that towards the hour of nones the wind fell in great part ; they hoisted a sail and took their bearings along the land and the galley came to an island that is called Barbarac. The captain's galley rode there and cast anchor ; the crew had great need of rest. It was already the hour of vespers and the sun was going down. Thither too came one of the galleys of Messire Charles ; it was the one they had sighted at dawn ; but it was fifteen days before all five ships were once more together. It pleased God that none of them should perish ; and all thus going in search of the captain in the divers ports of Brittany, ended by finding themselves together. The men on each ship imagined that the other galleys had gone down : great therefore was their joy when they saw Pero Niño, Messire Charles and all their other comrades. Certain knights of Brittany came to visit them, and the captain had his tent set up in the island and invited them all to eat with him and gave them a most noble feast. Each recounted the adventures that had befallen him during the night of the tempest. Messire Charles said that his galley climbed into the clouds and dropped into the abyss ; that sometimes she went with head aloft and sometimes head down ; that he thought so much about his soul that the world no

longer mattered to him ; and that the sea had carried
away everything upon the deck up to the oarsmen's
benches, which for the moſt part had been torn out.
His shipmaſter told that so many and so ſtrong were
the blows of the waves againſt his galley that they
nearly capsized her ; that many times he thought he
saw the decks go under and the keel come atop ; and
that once he saw the ſtars in the sky between the deck
and the hull of the galley. He likewise said that his
galley would have been opened by the force of the waves
if he had not had her frapped with cables and mats.⁷⁴
Others said that several men had died stifled in the
hold, so close pressed were they therein.

Each thus recounted the toils and labours that he
had had to endure. The captain said to them : " My
friends, we owe many thanks to God who has delivered
us. We had to pass through this trial and God has
saved us that we may do some good. Let us try to
make up for loſt time." He further said : " See how
God protects this evil nation of the English. He
protects them not because they are righteous but
because of our sins, for if they are evil, we are sinful.
If God was this time againſt us, yet another time we
shall find Him favourable, for He is full of mercy,
and if we have found the sea enraged, another time
we shall see her kind. Let no man, therefore, despair ;
men should know how to endure evil fortune ; man is
born to labour. Those who have conquered lands
and won kingdoms have had to go through many
hardships and bear heavy labours." When Pero Niño
had finished his discourse, Messire Charles said that
these were words of a good knight and that all should

be done as he should order. As soon as the feasting was ended, they set to work to mend the galleys and to provision them with everything needful, and then the mariners observed the weather and the wind. The galleys set out thence and had a calm sea and a good wind for their passage. They sailed under the great sail and mizzensail, rowing at times for a day and a night. The next morning England was sighted and by the hour of vespers they had drawn in close to the land. There were along the coast many boats out fishing; the galleys captured a few of them. Through them they were able to get information and to ascertain the state of the country and of each place.

The land which the galleys approached is called the country of Cornwall; and as soon as they had information about this country the galleys made their way to the shore with the tide, up a river.[75] This river is so swift at its mouth and so dragged the galleys that there were neither oars nor rudders that could have stopped them nor guided them until they had got out of this current. And this current was as long as a cross-bowshot: when they had got out of it, the oars could make themselves felt. Within there was a harbour, well sheltered and shielded from every wind, and a town which is called St Ives,[76] having perhaps about three hundred inhabitants. This town was not fortified; it was set out in terraces on the slope of a hill and all the streets went down to the sea. There the galleys drew in to land. The town was very rich, for they were all merchants and fishermen who dwelt there. The captain ordered all his men to arm ; they threw down gangways and all landed with the captain, who drew up his troop in good order. He set in the front a pavisade,[77] and behind it the crossbowmen. The captain and Messire Charles joined forces and arrayed them by mutual agreement. There was a rough fight there ; at the laſt the English were driven in and many among them killed or taken. The captain commanded that the ſtandards and the men at arms should remain in good array outside the town, so that they should not be surprised if the English came up in greater force, and that the oarsmen and crossbowmen should enter the city to sack it, the ones fighting and the others plundering. When everything had been carried off he set fire to the town and burnt it all : all this was done in the space of three hours. The trumpets sounded : everyone went back on board and the galleys set out again, taking with them two sailing ships that were in the port. The tide then began to fall and the galleys went out on the ebb and towed the ships out of the current. When they were at the mouth of the harbour, many English were already gathered together there and the passage had become very narrow ; on one side there was a very high rock which towered above the galleys and there fell on them from either shore a hail of ſtones and arrows, and if the English had been gathered together at the firſt in as great numbers as they were then, the descent on shore would have been very perilous, although the crossbowmen had given them-selves no respite. That night the captain manned the

captured ships with sailors and all that was needful
and ordered them to set sail for France to the port of
Harfleur.[78] And Pero Niño and Messire Charles
agreed to the plan of going along round the coast
of England. They came to a great seaport which is
called Dartmouth.[79] All over the countryside they
saw fair troops of soldiers and archers coming up on
all sides to defend the shore. And the captain said
to Messire Charles : " There is a fair place for a fight,
and what is more, we have need of water : let us go
against those men." Messire Charles answered : " My
lord, there are more men there than you have : it is
not a good place for so few men as we are." Whereupon they had that day, on the question of this landing,
some words of discord. This was the place where the
English had killed Messire Guillaume du Chastel,[80]
and the captain said that because Messire Guillaume
had died there, that was no reason that everyone else
who went ashore there should die. " Every one goes
to market with his own luck ; all go to make a profit,
therefore it happens to each according to luck and fate.
It is the same in wars ; each thinks to win, but afterwards it befalls as God has ordained. We likewise
do not know His secrets ; but with His help and with
a good plan men should go bravely to their business ;
for he who fears everything had better not go out of
his own house. It is neither embroideries, nor furs,
nor chains, nor cloak-clasps that make war, but hard
fists and determined men."

.   .   .

When the captain Pero Niño and Messire Charles
were of one accord again as they had been heretofore,

the galleys set out from Dartmouth and kept out at sea all night, in great fear of meeting with the English fleet. When day broke they rowed along the coaſt to Plymouth.[81] This is a good town, set on a height above the sea ; on the land side it is not so high, but there is a good fortress on a little mound. There is no means of landing there if resiſtance is offered, unless the landing is made far from the town ; and once ashore it is not difficult to capture. It is on the banks of a river, a bolt-shot from the sea. There is a bridge there, made like the bridge of Seville of boats, in which there may be some seven or eight boats. There were many sailing ships or other vessels lying in the river, but as soon as they sighted the galleys, they were all hauled up close the bridge. The galleys entered the river to take some of these ships and burn them. They fired so many bombards and bolts from the town, that those in the galleys thought they would be sunk ; there was one ſtone which went twice the height of a tower and fell into the sea nearly half a league off ; so that they could not capture any ship. The galleys drew off thence along the coaſt. One morning they found themselves crossing a gulf that is called the Casquet[82] ; there are there rocks of great height between which there is no passage and no man knows of one. A ſtrong wind began to blow from the sea full upon the galleys and drove them by force upon the rocks. It availed naught to row ; there was nothing to be done but to call upon the Virgin Mary for succour. The galleys gave themselves up for loſt. Moreover the current was so ſtrong that it drew them continually towards the gulf ; but it pleased God that this current which drew them into the gulf at one end should send them out at the other, which was a great marvel, and all gave thanks to God. Thereafter, by dint of rowing, and against the wind, they drew away from the land and reached the open sea. In that place have many ships perished. That night they passed at sea ; the next day, they came to an island which is called Portland.[82] It is a little island, quite close to the coast of England. At low tide, men pass from one to the other : at high tide they cross in boats. This island is round and girt with tall rocks which leave no entry except on the side facing the land. It contains a township in which dwell about two hundred inhabitants.

The captain Pero Niño sent some of his men with his standard to sack this town and carry off the flocks on the island : and Messire Charles did likewise. They themselves remained with the rest of their men, hoping that when the tide went down some English troops might appear. Those who went on the island fought for a while with those they met ; but these were all ill-armed and few in number and soon took to flight. There were many caverns in the rocks near the sea-shore, very great, which were entered down narrow little paths ; and these paths so wound about that a single man could defend the steps of one of these passages. And the townsfolk had seen the galleys earlier, when they were skirting round the island, and for the most part had taken refuge in the caverns with their wives and children, so that very few of them could be taken prisoners and our men had to fall back on plundering the township. While our men were on the island, the trumpets sounded on board the galleys to recall every one to the ship. Then the French who were in the company began to set fire to the houses, and the Castillians would not have it done ; instead they hindered them from doing it more, as the people of the island were poor. Indeed, a miracle was wrought there ; which was that a Castillian set fire to a house roofed with thatch, and that the fire took no hold at all, because the Castillian did not light it willingly ; but as for the French, as soon as they set fire to a house, it was consumed. That was the reason why the Castillians had no heart to ravage the town further, having pity on the poor folk. Well they knew that such was the desire of their captain, ever gentle to the weak and strong against the strong. So our men took their way back to the galleys, and by the time they reached them, many English men at arms and bowmen had already crossed over with the ebb. The captain Pero Niño and Messire Charles were already engaged with the English ; these fought to cross over to the defence of the island, for they saw there the men from the galleys, while our men fought to prevent their passage. The number of the English grew with every minute ; and as the Captain had not time enough to fight so as to bar the passage, as the tongue of sand was wide, while they were engaged with some, others slipped by on to the island. The men who were marching with the captain's banner had reached the high part of the island, and thence they saw the fight and that many men were coming against them. They

set themselves in good array (for there were brave folk
among them) haſtened their ſteps, went to meet the
English and threw themselves upon them very roughly;
but the English ſtood firm. There were thus two
conflicts very close to each other. Those who came
from the island drove in the English line and forced
them back as far as the other conflict, so that there
was only one battle. Messire Charles went into the
battle leading his men and fighting like a good knight.
He had with him his ſtandard and the moſt part of
his men. The captain took his ſtandard, which had
been brought back from the island, rallied his men,
had a pavisade set before his crossbowmen and called
near him his cousin Fernando Niño and his men at
arms. He said to them : " Look at the French, they
are fighting like brave men, and can do no more. We
muſt bring them help, for they are engaged with so
many that they can no longer offer resiſtance. It is
for you to aid them." So speaking they went againſt
the English and attacked them fiercely with darts and
with arrows; and the captain came up with his
banner. There was there a fierce fight in a very small
space. In the end the English had to give up their
position, little as they liked it, and withdraw to the
mainland. At this moment the tide came in, and
separated the combatants from each other. This was
the cause of the Englishmen's quick withdrawal, for
they saw the tide making, and thought that if their
retreat were cut off, they had nothing to hope for but
death, so desperate was the battle that the French and
the Caſtillians waged againſt them. But these, if the
tide had not risen, could no longer have gone on

resisting them, so great was the number of enemies that came against them. The land which was covered again by the tide was as wide as a stone can be thrown from the hand ; and the English from the other side sent so many stones and arrows that it seemed as if it snowed, and a great quantity reached those who were on the island. The captain that day made some fair shots with the crossbow, wherewith he overthrew and wounded many of the English ; and this exchange of arrows lasted for a long time, until night brought it to an end. Our men withdrew to their galleys, tended their wounded, ate and rested. That day they took a few prisoners.

On the morrow the galleys left there and went along the coast seeking the ports. Men from the galleys landed to get water and wood, and seeing herds of cows and sheep they laid hands on them and killed as many as they needed. So they went along the coast, each day burning and pillaging many houses, carrying off goods and apparel ; and they had frequent skirmishes with those who dwelt in those parts. As they thus went along the captain heard of a township called Poole[84] which is on that coast. This town belonged to a knight called Harry Paye,[85] a Corsair who was always voyaging with many ships, capturing all that he could of the vessels of Spain and France. And this Harry Paye had many times come to the coasts of Castille, whence he had carried off many boats and ships : he cruised in the Flanders Channel with such powerful forces that no ship could pass into Flanders without being taken. This Harry Paye had burnt Gijon and Finisterre and carried off the crucifix of St Mary of Finisterre, which was famous as that held in the most devotion in all the country (this was true, for I have seen it), and he wrought much other havoc in Castille, taking there many prisoners to hold them to ransom; and although other armed ships came forth out of England, it was he who the most often made folk talk of him. When the captain learned that he was so near his home, he rejoiced greatly thereat, thinking to find him there, and one morning, at dawn, the galleys appeared before Poole. This town was not walled: it had a fair tower with a round leaden roof shaped like a cup. The captain told Messire Charles that it would be well to land here at this spot and to go to sack and burn the town. Messire Charles answered: "My lord, my counsel is that we should not land here, because there are many shoals and reefs, and the galleys cannot get close in to the shore; and there are in this place many men at arms and bowmen." The captain said: "We will land in the long boats a few at a time, and while some fight, the rest will be coming ashore." Messire Charles answered that the captain might do as he liked, but that not for anything in the world would he and his men go ashore. Then the captain armed his men, and landed them, bidding them fire the town. This town of Poole is some distance from the sea. The Castillians set fire to it and burnt a great part of it; but so many English came against them, that they could not make a stand against them, but withdrew slowly and in good order towards the sea. The captain, seeing his men giving way and leaving the town, was much vexed and ordered more men to land ; meanwhile the others fought and defended themselves until the reinforcements came up. Fernando Niño, the captain's cousin, led these and had with him the standard and the men at arms ; he ranged his men and gave the order to go back and destroy the town. They set out well together to reach it according to their leader's command. The banner was set outside the town, with the men at arms round it. The captain had ordered that they should take no plunder, for fear that the soldiers should be hampered by the booty, but that they should set fire to everything. So in a little time the town was altogether burnt, except for one fair and great dwelling, which was defended by many men who had taken refuge therein ; but the Castillians were so determined that they forced an entrance into this house also, and those who were within escaped by the back; they found therein a quantity of all manner of arms, bolts, rigging, sails and all the furnishings of ships-of-war. They carried off as much as they could of these things and then fired the castle. This affair ended, they came back towards the galleys, still fighting with the English ; and as they began to board the galleys there came up a great number of English on foot and on horseback. The horsemen dismounted, went forward on foot, and made a fair array of men at arms and bowmen ; and they were so near them that they could easily tell the fair men from the dark. They had with them house doors, which they set upon the ground, propping them up on ſtakes and sheltering behind them in the battle. They did this for fear of the arbaleſts, which used to kill many of them. They held the higher ground and the Caſtillians the lower ; and the arrows were so many and came so thick that the crossbowmen did not dare to ſtoop to bend their bows. Many were already hit by these arrows, and there were so many, that those who wore leather jerkins or surcoats seemed all ſtuck with arrows. The ſtandard and he who bore it were likewise riddled with arrows, and the ſtandard bearer had as many round his body as a bull in the ring, but he was well shielded by his good armour, although this was already bent in several places. The English are experienced in war and, to get to grips with the Caſtillians they waited until the crossbowmen should, by dint of shooting, have emptied their trusses.

The captain Pero Niño was in his galley, whence he saw how the number of the English grew every moment and that there were among them many valiant men at arms. He recognised that the issue hung in the balance ; he left his galley with the small company that had ſtayed there and landed. Messire Charles, when he saw the captain go ashore, made ready to go to his help, although it was already late. When the Caſtillians saw the captain they took fresh courage. He, encouraging all he met, reached his ſtandard. He who bore it was alone and in great jeopardy between the Caſtillians and the English, for, to declare the truth, the Caſtillians had retreated some three paces which the English had gained. Well do soldiers know that all have their eyes on the banner, enemies as well as friends ; and if its men see it retreat

in the battle, they lose heart, while the enemies
courage waxes ; and if they see it ſtand firm or go
forward, they do the same. But neither because the
ſtandard bearer is granted such an honour, and has
been chosen out of the whole army to fill this office,
nor because all look to him and have their eyes upon
him, muſt it happen that pride and vanity wax within
him, and that he ascribe to himself a greater part than
has been assigned to him, that he march more in the
van than has been ordered, or that he think that his
charge has been given to him as being the moſt valiant
man in that army. He muſt tell himself that many
other and better men are round him and that it is
they that do the work. Let him not wish to diſtinguish
himself and excel another in honour, so that in the
end he endangers the honour of his maſter and those
who follow him ; neither let him keep himself so far
behind that the reſt advance and he remains in the
rear ; for a candle gives more light when it is borne
before than behind, and the ſtandard is like a torch
set in a room to give light to all men ; if by some
accident it is put out, all remain in darkness
and unseeing and are beaten. And so for such an
office should there be chosen a man of great sense,
who has already been seen in great affairs, who has good
renown and who on other occasions has given a good
account of himself. Such a work should be given
neither to a presumptuous man, nor to a haſty man,
for he who is not maſter of himself cannot lead others.
And some to whom this office has been entruſted have
brought their maſters and those who follow them into
evil ſtraits, since the lord has bidden his men follow

the banner. Great reason is there to reproach that lord who sets his men under such a ſtandard-bearer, for honour so works upon gentlefolk that it drives them into certain danger. So it is fitting that the ſtandard-bearer should conform to the will of his lord and should not do more than he is ordered. And Pero Niño said to Gutierre Diaz, his ſtandard-bearer : " Friend, take heed when you hear the trumpets sound ; then march forward with the ſtandard and go forward up to the English. There make your ſtand and leave it not." The captain, very well armed, as soon as he had arrayed his men, ſtarted shouting with a loud voice : " Saint James ! Saint James ! " The trumpets sounded, the ſtandard advanced and all rushed after it. Then was it time for every man to do his duty and to shew his worth, for no man lacked an adversary. The battle was well suſtained on both sides ; at laſt the English gave way, but not all, for the gentlefolk fought very ſteadily as they retreated. If the men from the galleys who were on foot had been mounted, they could have made many men prisoners that day ; even as it was enough were killed or taken. At this moment, Messire Charles came ashore, leading many knights and gentlemen in armour ; they appeared in another part of the field, richly apparelled in surcoats and other ornaments of gold and silver. And I speak truth : when the battle was ended the arrows lay so thick upon the ground that no man could walk without treading on arrows in such numbers that they picked them up in handfuls. It happened that the one man from Messire Charles' galley who came up in time to fight, died : he was a

Caſtillian, and a brave man; he was called Juan de Murcia. That day there died also a brother of Harry Paye, a good soldier, who did very fair deeds before he died. When all was over, Pero Niño invited Messire Charles to dine with him that day, he and his knights; and so was it done. And in such sort had the English been beaten and vanquished that not one of them appeared again, but they let the Caſtillians get aboard their galleys again at their ease, without a conflict. These tended their wounded, and ate and reſted, for they had need to. And then Messire Charles said to the captain[86]: "My lord, you muſt forgive me, for these knights were overlong in arming themselves and while I awaited them I did not bring you aid in this battle; wherefore the honour is all yours, and I have no part in it." The captain answered: "My lord, another time you will do better; and if were mine to give, I would give you all the honour of this battle, for I know you to be so good a knight that you can do no wrong wheresoever you may be."

The captain there learnt that the King of England had brought together a great army, and had taken many folk from that part to march againſt Owen, Prince of Wales, who had rebelled againſt him.

.   .   .

The captain and Messire Charles held counsel with their mariners as to what they should do thenceforward. And the pilots and the maſters of the oarsmen said: "My lords, ye have been long enough upon these coaſts and have done many fine things here; you carry away from this land much honour and likewise profit. We are at the beginning of winter. These seas are very ſtormy, and especially evil for galleys, and it is time that ours should be repaired : they lack many things that they have loſt in the gales. Moreover this country is very cold and men suffer here if they be not warmly clad. Our counsel is that you leave England and that you go to winter in some port of France." All agreed that the counsel was good and that it muſt be followed ; but the captain said that firſt he wished to go to set his eyes on London ; and he ordered them to set their course for it. The galleys came to a port which is called Southampton,[87] close to London. They found there a Genoese carrack, which the English had taken in the Flanders Channel. The galleys captured her, but she was empty, and wished to carry her off, but she had no sails. The captain ordered that she should be fired ; then the carrack's boat came up, manned by Genoese, who begged the captain of his grace to spare them, since he well knew that the Genoese were servants and friends of the king of Caſtille ; that this carrack had been taken from them by the English, although they had a safe-conduċt from the King of England ; that they had pleaded their cause before the King, and he had ordered that she should be given back to them and that now she was theirs. And the captain, knowing the truth, left them their carrack.

They saw London lying in a plain[88] : it is a great city, and thence to the open sea it muſt be two leagues. There comes there from the north a great river which encircles the land on which it ſtands, the which is

called the Thames.[89]   There is on the other side an
island, which is called the Isle of Wight;[90] the part of
this island which is next the sea is covered with thick
forests and is very flat. The captain landed some
shield-bearers and crossbowmen to reconnoitre the
country ; but in an instant so many archers appeared
that the little troop turned very quickly back to the
sea. Other men then landed from the galleys, and
skirmished a moment with the English ; but these
came up in such numbers that they had to go on board
again. This island is rich. They say that as many as
fifteen hundred men dwell there and that the most
of them are archers ; and indeed as they went along
the coast they saw many men.

The galleys left there, and set their course for
Harfleur, which is in France.

.   .   .

When the galleys reached Harfleur, they were well
received ; and their men, as well as the captain, were
well pleased. Harfleur is a fair city and a good port
at high tide. The ships come into the city by the
mouth of a river that runs through the midst of it.
The sea skirts half the city and on the other half there
is a good wall and very strong towers, with a very fair
moat made with stone and lime, filled with water.
The entrance is by drawbridges and double gates :
each gate is between two very strong towers. This
city is always well furnished and rich in merchandise,
making much fine cloth. A league off is Montivillier,[91]
a good town where there is a noted convent of nuns.
They weave there much fine stuff. At that place
there runs into the sea a great and famous river which

is called the Seine ; there is no greater river in France, above the Race. From thence to Paris is fifty leagues along the ſtream ; and carts[92] and boats come and go from that town to Paris. In the city of Harfleur the captain and his men were lodged for some days. While Pero Niño was there, there came thither Martin Ruiz de Avendaño, captain of the sailing ships of Caſtille. The captain Pero Niño explained his conduct to him and told him that he seemed to have no heed to the service of the King of Caſtille. The words between them were so ſtrong that much harm might have befallen them. Pero Niño told him that he had not acted as a good knight should, and that he would make him know it ; but the French liked Pero Niño, and would not let matters go further ; but the two parted enemies.

The captain and Messire Charles forgot the toils they had endured, alike on sea and in the wars they had waged, in the good fortune they had had together againſt the English, and they resolved to go once more to England. They made ready their galleys and provisioned them ; and three other whaling-boats of France, furnished for war, joined the captain.

They set out, and passed the night under the cape of Caux. In the dawn watch they set their course to England and unfurled their sails ; but when they reached the open sea, as they came into the Channel, they found the wind and the ſtorm so violent that they were near sinking ; and they broke several lateen yards and other rigging. All this was but natural, for it was already winter ; and they were forced, much against their will, to return to the port of Harfleur. There they remained, guarding the coast, as the English fleet came very often to plunder the port and to land to do much harm. But all the time that Pero Niño was there, no English fleet appeared. He remained there so long that his men could no longer endure the cold and the great rains, for there is always much rain on the coasts of this sea.

As it was no longer possible to cross to England by reason of the heavy squalls, it was resolved to go up the Seine in the galleys and to winter in Rouen, a very noble city which is on the banks of this stream, well furnished with all the things of which they had need. So they began to go up the stream, which has very fair banks, where may be seen many good villages and many fair houses of great lords. Beside the stream there is an abbey of Benedictine monks, very rich and held in much honour, and many lovely woods and gracious orchards and gardens. And the lords of this country came to see the captain and feasted him nobly. So the galleys came to the city of Rouen. The King of France had there on the other side of the river an arsenal which held galleys and great horse-boats,[93] which are very great galleys that can take horses and many men to sea. The captain was lodged in Rouen in a great hostelry, very fair, and his men in other inns near him.

The French are a noble nation; they are wise, understanding, and delicate in all matters that pertain to good breeding, courtesy and nobility. They are most fine in their dress and magnificent in their equipment; they have their own fashions, which are

peculiar to them[94] ; they are generous and great givers
of presents ; they like to give pleasure to everyone ;
they treat ſtrangers moſt honourably ; they know how
to praise and praise fair deeds much ; they are not
mischievous and give shelter even to the wearisome[95] ;
they demand satisfaction of no man in word or in deed,
unless it greatly concern their honour. They are moſt
courteous and gracious in their speech ; they are very
gay, gladly giving themselves up to pleasure, and
seeking it. They are very amorous, as well women as
men, and proud of it. Here the author says that these
qualities come naturally to them and that they glorify
themselves for being gay and amorous, because this
country lies in the clime of a ſtar that is called Venus,
and that this clime is under this gay and amorous
planet. None the less, though the people of this
country explain these things according to what they
have heard of this art of aſtrology, which is *motus et
fertus*, the matter is grave and judgment difficult, since
God is at the same time Nature and above Nature and
againſt Nature, when it pleases Him to receive the
prayers and petitions of the righteous, and even of the
unrighteous when they turn to Him. Often the planet
or the sign is conſtrained not to exercise its influence,
for He who made laws can revoke them. Our Lord
God has made many things, but He has made none
contrary to His power. So soon as Lucifer pretended
to be as mighty as God, neither the heavens nor the
sun nor moon nor all the other ſtars could prevent his
falling into the middle of the earth (although the
middle of the earth could not, according to Nature,
receive him) because this place was given and assigned

him as a place of endless punishment for him and his like.

The captain lived familiarly with the knights and gentlemen of France, as a man who had been nurtured and brought up in all nobleness. He soon learnt the fair manners of the nation ; for, as says the philosopher, for one man a short lesson is enough, while for another long teaching profits not. And the philosopher says this, because he to whom something has been given by Nature makes easy progress therein. To Pero Niño all good learning and all courtesy came by Nature, and ever did he use them so long as he lived ; and the fame thereof endures to this day, and shall ever endure among knights and nobles. He equipped himself very finely, according to the fashion of the country, and as befitted him, with the intent of going to Paris. There dwelt near Rouen a noble knight, who was named Messire Renaud de Trie,[96] Admiral of France, who was old. He sent to beg the captain to come to see him ; and the captain left Rouen and went to a place called Serifontaine,[97] where the admiral lived. And the Admiral welcomed him greatly and asked him to remain with him and to reſt himself for some days, for he had been much wearied by the sea ; and there the captain reſted for three days. The Admiral was a knight old and ill ; he was broken by his armour, for he had always fought and had been a ſtern knight in war ; and now he could no longer frequent either court or camp. He lived in retirement on his lands :

there he was richly furnished in all things needful for his person, and he dwelt in a house, plain and ſtrong, arranged and equipped as if it had been in the city of Paris. He had there with him his squires and his servants for every kind of office, as befits such a lord. In this house was a very fair chapel, where mass was said every day; and minſtrels and trumpeters who sounded their inſtruments marvellously. A river flowed before the house, on the banks of which were orchards and gracious gardens. On the other side was a pool full of fish, surrounded by walls and locked with a key, from which each day they could take fish enough for three hundred people; and when they wished to catch fish they held back the water so that it did not run into the pool, and they opened a conduit by which all the water was drawn off, so that the pool was dry: then they took the fish they needed and left the reſt and opened the upper conduit and in a little while the pool was filled. And this lord had forty or fifty hounds for hunting in the woods and men to tend them. He had there as many as twenty mounts for himself, among which were coursers, war-horses, jouſting horses[98] and hackneys. What more shall I tell you? Every sort of provision, every commodity was to be found there. He had, near the house, foreſts wherein were found all manner of game, both great and small, and with the forty or fifty hounds that he kept he hunted the ſtag, the doe and the boar, that in Spain is called *xabali*.[99] He had *neblis* falcons, which in French are called gentle, to hunt by the river, and very good herners. This knight had for wife the moſt beautiful lady then in France. She came of the greateſt family

135

and the beſt lineage of Normandy and was the daughter of the Lord of Bellengues. Much was she praised for all the things that pertain to a great lady ; and as she had great sense, she ruled her house better and kept it in better order than any other great lady of those parts. She had her own noble dwelling, apart from that of the Admiral ; a drawbridge crossed from one to the other and both were within one rampart. The furnishings of this dwelling were so many and of so outlandish a sort, that it would be long to recount them. She had as many as ten damsels of noble birth, moſt richly dressed and entertained, who had charge of nothing but of their own persons and to bear their lady company : for there were besides many other maids in her chamber.

I will recount to you the order and rule that the lady followed. In the morning, after she had risen, the lady went with her damsels to a grove, which was near there, each with her Book of Hours and her rosary. They seated themselves apart one from the other and said their Hours, and spoke not until they had finished prayers. Thereafter, picking flowers and violets as they went, they came back to the Caſtle and went to the Chapel where they heard a low Mass. Coming out thence, they took a plate of silver on which were chickens, larks, and other birds roaſted, and ate, and left as much as they would, and then they were given wine. My lady ate but rarely in the morning or only took a few trifling things to please those in her company. That done, Madam rode with her ladies on the beſt harnessed and fineſt hackneys that could be found, and with her rode any knights and gentlemen who

PLATE IV

THE PLEASURES OF A COUNTRY HOUSE VISIT

(Chasse à la cour de Philippe le Bon). Burgundian School. Musée Condé, Chantilly

might happen to be there ; and they rode for some time in the country, making chaplets of flowers. Then could be heard lays, *deslais,* virelays, roundelays, complaints and ballads and songs, of all the kinds which the French compose,[100] sung by voices diverse and well attuned. I declare to you that if a man who was there could have made it laſt for ever he would have wished for no other Paradise.

Thither came, with his gentlemen, the captain Pero Niño, for whom all these rejoicings were made ; and in like manner they came back to the Caſtle at the hour of dinner, dismounted and came into the hall, where they found the table laid. The good old knight could no longer ride, but he received his gueſts with such graciousness that it was marvel. He was a moſt gracious knight, although he was in so miserable a case. The Admiral, my Lady, and Pero Niño took their places at the high table, and the ſteward presided over the other table, and caused a knight or squire to sit beside each lady ; so was each seated. The viands, moſt varied, in great number and finely dressed, were of all sorts, meat, fish and fruits, according to the day. So long as the meal laſted any man who, with due measure and respeᴄt of courtesy, could speak of arms and love, was sure of finding someone to whom to address himself, and sure that he would be heard and answered as his desire would have it. During the repaſt there were players, making pleasant music upon divers inſtruments. Grace said, and the tables removed, the minſtrels came in, and my Lady danced with Pero Niño, and each of his gentlemen with a lady. This dance laſted for an hour. When it was ended

my Lady kissed Pero Niño, and each man the lady
with whom he had danced. Thereafter they brought
in spices, served wine and everyone went to his siesta.
The captain Pero Niño withdrew to his chamber in
my Lady's house, which was most fairly furnished and
called the tower room.[101] After the siesta, they
mounted their horses, and the pages came up with the
falcons. Herons had already been tracked down. My
Lady took her place, a falcon gentle on her wrist; the
pages beat up the game and she let her falcon fly at it
so gracefully and well that it could not have been better
done. You would have seen good hunting and great
sport, dogs swimming, drums beating, lures waving[102]
and ladies and gentlemen beside the river, enjoying
such delight as suffers not description. When they
had finished beating the valley, my Lady and all the
world with her dismounted in a meadow; there fowls,
cold partridges and fruits were brought to them and
all ate and drank and made chaplets of greenery; then
singing most delightful songs, they went back to the
Castle.

At nightfall there was supper, if it were winter.
If it were summer, they ate later and afterwards my
Lady went to seek distraction afoot in the country
and they played bowls until night fell, and thereafter
went back to the hall by torchlight; and then came
the minstrels. They danced far into the night; then
after fruits and wine had been served, they took their
leave and went to bed. This order which I have told
you was observed every day, according to the season,
whenever the captain or others came there, according
to their estate. All these matters were directed and

set in order by this lady; and likewise she governed all other matters both within and without; for the Admiral was a rich man, lord of many manors, and having great revenues; but he had to concern himself with none of these matters, the lady being capable of directing them all.

And if, through dear delights and abundance in all things, a man might always live and escape death, the Admiral would have done it; for so richly was he provided that no man of his rank could be better; but when the tale of the months which Job says that God has given to each is told, there are neither divinations, nor delights, nor riches, nor friends, nor kindred which sustain. And Pero Niño was so much loved, in all honour, by my Lady for the prowess that she beheld in him, that already she began to speak to him somewhat concerning his affairs, and asked him to go to see her father, a noble knight who was called Messire de Bellengues, who lived in Normandy. Pero Niño departed thence, and set forth for Paris. In every place where he passed, the knights came to receive him and did him great honour, having heard of his renown.

The King of France[103] was afflicted with madness; sometimes his reason returned to him, and he had his senses again, but when he began to give orders and to go out of his house, the madness came back and at once they laid hands on him and shut him up anew. Such was his life.

Pero Niño went to see the Dukes[104] and was well

received by them and by all the knights and gentlemen of the Court, who took pleasure in his company, and gave him a moſt honourable welcome and greatly sought him out at all the feaſts and feſtivals. It was written in the treaties and conventions of brotherhood which were between France and Caſtille, that each time that one of these kingdoms should send to ask aid of the other, it should grant it in the form agreed : the kings of these two countries could not have excused themselves, without very great penalties and without breaking their oaths, defaming their honour and their souls, from giving the support that was asked of them. And the kingdom which was thus succoured had to make a payment, according to the number of men who were sent and the length of time they remained there. The captain Pero Niño had already spent the pay that he had received from Caſtille. One day he came into the council, where were the Dukes, and with them King Louis and the King of Navarre and many other counts and great lords, and he asked that pay should be given him for his galleys. But whether because the councillors of the king were not agreed, or whether they did not wish to grant it, they dragged out the affair for a long time and gave him nothing, so that he found himself in danger of letting his galleys be laid up for want of money ; which would have happened if there had not been certain merchants who made him a loan on the security of his word. At laſt he spoke very ſtrong words in the council, and among other things said that since the king was ill and the council governed in his ſtead, in not observing the treaties and conventions exiſting between the kings of the two countries, the councillors were breaking the pacts and incurring the penalties which were there prescribed. Wherefore, they were committing an infraction *in lege*: *crimen majeſtatis*, and were breaking their oaths, which he did not believe that their lord the king would ever have done, if he had been of sound mind and in his senses; and that if any one would say the contrary, he would make him know it at once, hand to hand, before them. Whereupon, though they gave him to underſtand that he was using very ſtrong words, none the less they were of enough service for the council to ordain forthwith that all his expenses should be paid him; and there was no man there who answered him aught and there was no cause to do so, for he was in the right. After this, the Duke of Orleans sent to ask him not to press this matter, because the council had many other great affairs to dispatch, but that he would take heed that he was well paid and that for love of him and because he was a good knight he would do his beſt for him. The Duke of Burgundy for his part said as much, but the Duke of Orleans said further: " I would that you were of my household so long as you remain in France; and it matters not where you go, I will watch over your honour and your eſtate."

Pero Niño was greatly pleased thereat and answered: " I thank you much ", and seeing that all the affairs of France were in the hands of the Duke of Orleans, to get credit to fulfil the services of the king his maſter, he accepted the offers that had been made to him. The Duke gave him liveries and pay according to the French usage, and gave him the office of a chamberlain in his household. And the young and gallant knights of the Court looked at him, and said behind his back that this was the man who in such a place as the king's council had spoken such ſtrong words ; and they assumed badges and ordered jouſts to know what manner of knight he was and what was his worth. France lay then in great peace and in all its prosperity, although the evil had begun among them and the divisions between the dukes and the great lords of France, and one was already againſt the other.

.　　　.　　　.

The French jouſt after another fashion than that followed in Spain. They jouſt without liſts, and ſtrike after the fashion of war. They arm the horses with head pieces and petrels, which are armour made of very thick leather, and their saddles, likewise very ſtrong, cover their legs nearly to the feet. It often happens that one horse runs againſt another, and one falls, or that they both fall. It is a moſt perilous jouſting and one that all men do not attempt, but only those who are very skilful and very good horsemen. The ſtaves[105] are all of the same length ; there is in all the court only two or three craftsmen who make them, with the permission of the governors of the liſts, and they are sworn maſters. There is neither one that holds the liſts, nor jouſt of one man againſt another by champions assigned ; but each attacks whomsoever he will. All are assailants[106] ; ten, or twenty, or thirty, or more, take their place on one

side and as many on the other. As soon as one takes
his lance, the other at once grasps his ; and not only
one goes out againſt him, but in their great ardour it
happens that two or three come forward together
againſt him who has ſtood forth, notwithſtanding
their courtesy ; for if they see how the matter is going,
never againſt one man does more than one man come
forward. It is therefore needful that the knight who
jouſts there should be praĉtised therein, and should be
a ſtrong and moſt skilful horseman.

The French arranged jouſts one day, as a trial, at a
place meet for such matters that is called Little
Brittany.[107] On that day there jouſted the Count of
Clermont, the Count of la Marche, the Count of
Tonnerre, and other great men of the Court. That
day Pero Niño jouſted also, and ran many courses with
knights of renown, and broke many lances. Such was
the desire of the French to meet with him, that at one
time two knights came forward at once againſt him,
and ſtruck him at the same moment. But Pero Niño
ſtood so firm that they did not bear him from the
saddle, nor did he have any misadventure, nor lose
countenance at all, and a little after he overthrew a
good knight. That day the Count of Clermont and
a knight ran their horses againſt each other, which fell,
and both would have been dead, so rude was the shock,
if they had not been succoured at once.

There was held at that time in Paris a moſt
magnificent and noble marriage feaſt. It was made
by a majordomo of the king's, who was celebrating the
marriage of one of his daughters. There came to the
marriage the dukes, counts, great lords, and likewise the

143

knights and gentlemen of the court, the great ladies, ladies, maidens and damsels. The halls were moſt richly hung and the tables well ordered, each man in his place. There were there great and very rich vessels of gold and silver, and abundance of viands dressed in divers fashions. The company was so great that a town could have been peopled with the minſtrels alone, who played upon all kinds of inſtruments to make music, wind inſtruments and ſtringed, that are played with the hand or with a bow ; there were also choirs of voices. There were many dances, and rounds, and reels[108] ; and the ladies and the knights wore extraordinary adornments of so many fashions that they cannot be recounted for their number. The marriage-feaſt laſted for a whole week. When it was ended, the ladies gathered together and told the knights and the amorous gallants, that for love of their sweethearts they ought to make an honourable feſtival, in which they should jouſt in fair accoutrements, and that the ladies, at their own coſt, would have made a bracelet of gold, with a shield,[109] and a very rich chaplet, and that they would be there to look on to give them to the knight who should have done beſt. The knights rejoiced greatly thereat, for this thought held much to give them pleasure. They chose the place and day for the feſtival and the jouſt. While they waited until the day should come, they all assembled to make a trial in a place outside the city which is called the Couſture Sainte-Catherine.[110] Their fashion of making a trial is to jouſt one againſt the other, with as great force and as hard as each man beſt can, except that in these trials they wear neither surcoats nor crests ; they leave these for the festivals. It happens, moreover, that certain come to the trials who have no intent to joust at the festival : so did it happen that day for some. Pero Niño, who always preferred action to speech, thinking that he could not have better leisure, because of his weighty charge of the galleys, and since he was already near leaving again to begin to make war once more, took no heed of the festival but only of the trial. He had made ready two very gallant and good horses, which came from Castille ; one belonged to the Duke of Berri, the other to the High Constable, of whom he had asked them ; and he took a helm of noble fashion that had been sent to him by a great lady who was not at the festival. And that day there gathered together at the Cousture as many as a hundred knights or more, all in jousting armour ; and by the time Pero Niño got there, they had all begun to joust. The French, after they have run three or four courses, at once disarm. Pero Niño had brought many lances and pikes,[111] and set himself to joust against all comers, one after the other ; whosoever wished to joust at once found him ready. Of those who thus wished to measure themselves against him, from some he swept away the helm, from others he tore away the shield, from others he struck off some part of their armour and others he left hanging from their horses. Many lances were broken against him, and so long did Pero Niño stay in the tilt yard, and such fair deeds did he do there, that the rumour thereof ran through all the city, where they spoke of nought but of a Spaniard who had come to the joust and shewed himself so marvellous a knight, and

did so many valiant deeds. Then the moſt famous
jouſters that were at the court gathered together,
and sent a knight great in renown and great in ſtature,
called Jean de One. He came to the Couſture on a
ſtrong jouſting horse of great size ; and as he himself
was very tall, he appeared terrible in his armour. At
that the French once more became triumphant and
of good cheer. Pero Niño and he ran some fair courses
together with ſtrong lances, and Jean de One saw that
Pero Niño was so ſtrong a knight and so skilful, that he
could not claim the advantage over him. Then he
ran a course in which he ran at him full tilt, thinking
to overthrow him by the weight of his horse, after the
French manner. But the good knight, who ever knew
how to bring his affairs to a happy ending, had learnt
in the earlier encounters how his adversary was seeking
to unhorse him by maſtery, if he could ; so he held in
his horse a little, and when Jean de One would have
come upon him, he gave him the spurs and planted
his blow upon his adversary's shield. And at the
moment that he broke his lance the bodies of the two
horses met, and Jean de One and his horse rolled to
the ground. They ran up and lifted up the knight,
who had fallen in so rude a fashion that he was in peril
of death, and his horse with him. In this fall he
put his arm out of joint, and was for many days a
cripple.

This done, they sent into the field a German knight
called Sinque, a man famed in arms, a very good horseman, armed for the jouſt. He ran several courses
againſt Pero Niño, all trials of dexterity, for the
German never waited for the shock but made much

146

PLATE V

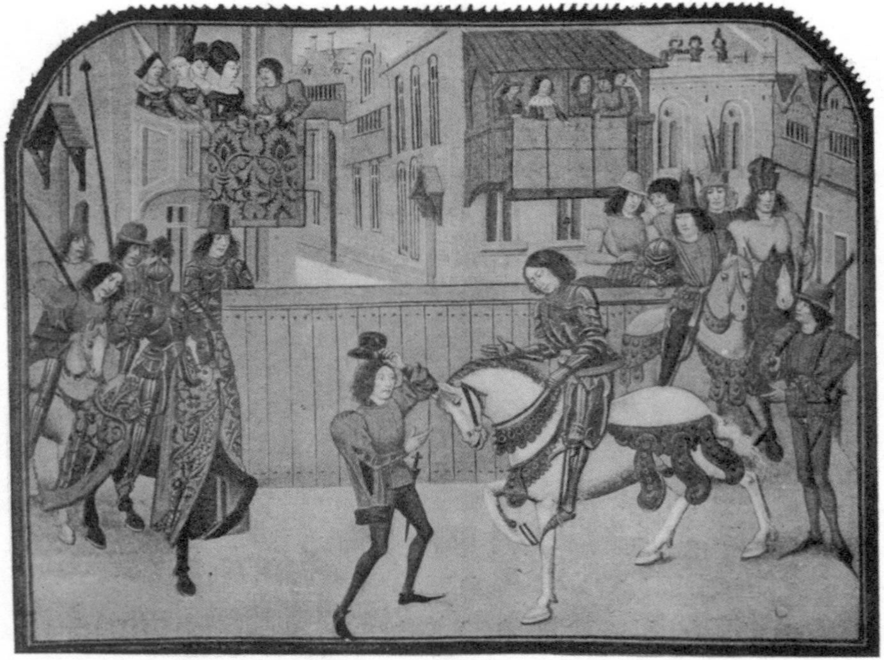

[Photo. Vromon

THE TILTYARD

From a miniature of the Histoire de Charles Martel. Brussels, Bibliothèque Royale de Belgique, MS. 6, fol. 51v

[face p. 146

play with the bridle of his horse, which he well knew how to do. He avoided the encounter, letting it pass, then nimbly wheeling round, came upon Pero Niño to reach him with the lance wherever he could, or else to get at him sideways with the petrel of his horse. Pero Niño saw plainly that this knight used artifice againſt him and did not wish to meet him full ; and as he also could use his bridle well, he knew perfeƈtly how to guard himself. The German always found him in front of him, however he might wheel, so that he could never escape under his lance ; it was a pretty thing to watch. At the end Pero Niño had the good fortune to get the German into such a position that he well believed he could not let him go. He ſtruck spurs into his horse, and ran at him ; but juſt in time the German wheeled, and took to flight as quickly as if his life had been in queſtion. Pero Niño did not follow him far; but thus galloping the German rode into the city gate and disappeared.

Thereupon, as the night was growing dark, Pero Niño ordered that they should take many torches and set them in line, like a ſtreet. Meanwhile gentlemen armed for jouſting arrived, but none of them took up a lance ; and they took off their helmets and ſtood by looking on. Then came up a gentle gallant who was much in love ; they told Pero Niño who he was, and he jouſted with him. At the second passage of arms, Pero Niño threw him, and his horse with him. The men afoot and the horsemen, who were there in great number, and kings at arms, and heralds and pursuivants, and trumpeters, and minſtrels, who were there in such multitude that no man could count, all gathered together round Pero Niño, and cried out three times : " The Captain of Spain holds the lists of La Cousture. Is there any man who comes against him ? " Thenceforward no more jousters appeared. Then all set themselves in array ; the torches went first, the servants picked up all the broken lances that lay in the field, and they went back into the city. The French are very courteous, and heartily praise him who does well. There was so great a crowd to watch that no man could go through the streets. They brought out from the houses torches and candles in such number that it was light as day. The noise of the minstrels, the trumpeters and the drummers was so loud that no man could hear a word. Pero Niño had not once taken off his helmet since he had donned it, and only removed it when he reached his chamber. When he doffed it there was such a press to see him that the coming and going of folk who wished to look at him lasted until midnight.

Thereafter Pero Niño was known to the whole court, and men held him in great account in all the seats of honour, and he was bidden to all the feasts that were given. They knew, moreover, that he belonged to one of the first twelve families of France, of those that are called the flower of France, of the house of Anjou, which is one of the branches of the royal house of France, and it bears the same arms as the Niños, which are or, semé of fleurs de lys azure ; and as there were kings of this lineage at Naples, nowadays they call by the name of Angevin those that there belong to the French party.

Pero Niño left there and set out for Rouen, where were his galleys and his men. In the midſt of all this died the good knight the Admiral of France, and my lady of Serifontaine sent to seek Pero Niño and told him all her affairs, and hence forward they held each other as lovers.

Here the author says : if it is true that men in love are more valiant and do greater deeds and are better men for the love of their sweethearts, what muſt he have been who had such a sweetheart as Jeannette de Bellengues, Madame de Serifontaine ! for there is neither king, nor duke, nor great lord in search of a lady to love who would not hold himself rich and happy to have a like sweetheart. All the virtues that true lovers have declared that their lady muſt have, all these had this lady in perfeƈtion, beautiful, and good, and young, and moſt pleasing, graceful and gay, and loved and witty ; such a lady might make her choice wheresoever she would. Moreover she was very rich and of great underſtanding. And they gave each other rich jewels.

While Pero Niño was at Rouen with his men, there was sent him a letter from Paris from six knights of the household of the Duke of Orleans. The letter, translated, said thus :

" Notre sire beau-frère, Mosen Pierre, Capitan d'Espana, les votres frères très-aimés chaballeires, que vos seront scriptes noſtres nomes seyllés, nous recomendons trois mill fués à vos, etc."[112]

This was the letter that the knight sent to Pero Niño.

" Our lord and fair brother, Messire Pierre, Captain of Spain, your well beloved brothers, the six knights whose names are writ beneath their seals, commend ourselves to you three thousand times. Already you know how Messire Ponce en Perellos bears the White Lady[113] embroidered on his apparel, and a golden bracelet, to despite the knights of my lord the duke of Orleans. He says that if there be seven knights who would fight against seven others, who shall defend this device, these are ready to enter the lists against them, and to fight to the very uttermost. Well know ye that we, thanks be to God, have held the tiltyard against the English, seven against seven, and have been left as victors. To us rather than to any others does it pertain to make answer to this challenge. But, blessed be always our Lord Jesus Christ, God hath willed that of the seven brothers who thus held the field against the English, one should have died. This was the noble knight Messire Guillaume du Chastel, whom God rest, who died as a good knight should, waging war in Cornwall. For this reason we beg you that for the honour of knighthood and the love of your lady, it should please you to be our brother in place of the good knight Messire Guillaume du Chastel, and one of those who should dispute this emprise.

" We send you this letter by Paris, King at Arms of our lord the king, in which and by which we beseech you to answer forthwith. The first of March. Messire Arnaut-Guillen de Barbasan, Champagne, Clignet de Brebant, amiral de France, Archambaut, Carrogier, and Messire Guillaume Bataille."[114]

When the letter had been read by the King at Arms, Pero Niño received it with great joy, and sent his answer to the knights, that read after this wise :

The Answer that Pero Niño gave to the King at Arms
" My lords, well-beloved friends and brothers, noble and valiant knights, I, Pero Niño, commend myself to the good graces of you all. I have seen a moſt gracious letter which it has pleased you to send me by Paris, King at Arms of my lord the king, in which you tell me of the feat and the emprise of the White Lady, and the public challenge of Messire Ponce en Perellos, and the end which he proposes ; and how you would accept his conditions and hold the tiltyard, seven againſt seven, as you have done once already and had the victory and been the vanquishers. Moreover, you have sent to me to ask me to take the place of the noble knight Messire Guillaume du Chaſtel, to be your brother and comrade in this encounter. Well-beloved lords, God knows that no tidings could reach me whereat I should feel greater joy than when I read your letter concerning this matter ; and I give you a hundred thousand graces and thanks for that you have wished to choose so young a man as I, and so little used to armour and tilt-yards, above all for a matter so high as this, and moreover to take the place of a knight so noble as was Messire Guillaume. Therefore to-day am I happier for your letter than I should be for the greateſt jewel that could be given me in the world ; henceforward hold me as your comrade and brother so long as I shall live ; and it pleases me and is my desire and I agree to accept it, and I accept moſt willingly this undertaking to the end of doing

therein all that I can, and God shall be my aid. If it please you that I should be there with you at the moment of challenging the device, or if you decide that I should challenge it for myself and at the same time for you, write to me at once, for I am ready to do it with all my heart."

When the knights saw Pero Niño's answer, they rejoiced greatly, and challenged the devices of Messire Ponce and his companions. Pero Niño thereupon came to the court to prepare himself for the tiltyard, and was well received in the household of the Duke and by his comrades, and there he busied himself over his armour and apparel and he had made a very rich surcoat embroidered with his arms. Then my lady of Serifontaine sent him by one of her kinsmen a horse and a helm and a letter in which she besought him most earnestly by his love for her that, if he had not already accepted a share in the conflict, he should not take any and that she would rejoice greatly thereat ; that if, however, it was a question greatly concerning his honour and he could not do otherwise, he should tell her what things he would need, and she would furnish them most fully, in such a fashion that he might advance his honour ; and therefore she sent him even now a horse, in case he had need of one, and that in all France he could not find a better for such work. Pero Niño accepted the horse for love of her, but sent to tell her that the conflict would not be on horseback.

The knights who were to enter the lists were preparing themselves when the king was informed of what was taking place, and of the discord which was already beginning ; he had all the knights engaged in the affair brought before him, and took away their devices, and reconciled the dukes and knights, and the dukes gave each other their devices. The Duke of Orleans gave to the Duke of Burgundy the hood with the porcupine that was his badge; the Duke of Burgundy gave the Duke of Orleans the badge of the joiner's plane with a diamond which was his device. I would explain to you the badges of these lords according to the meaning which each of them attached thereto. It was said that the *camal* of the Duke of Orleans signified *ca-mal*, that is : *combien de mal*, how much evil is done in these days. As for the porcupine, it is a gentle beaſt, but when anyone would harm it it becomes angry, and shoots its darts or quills and wounds sorely with them. The Duke of Burgundy had taken a carpenter's plane to signify that, juſt as a plane planes down all things, so could he overthrow all pride and arrogance ; as for the diamond which graves into ſteel and all other ſtones, while none can mark it, it signified that the duke was so mighty, that none would appear before him to demand satisfaċtion for aught that he did. The Duke of Berri, uncle of these two, had for his badge the figure of a bear, sitting and licking its paws, because the bear is a fierce beaſt that lives by itself, and if it be attacked, defends itself and even kills. The duke meant this to signify that he ſtayed quiet, living on his eſtates, doing evil to no one, but that if any would wrong him, he would defend himself and that he was mighty enough to fear no man. On this day of reconciliation the Duke of Berri, the Duke of Orleans, the Duke of Burgundy, and all the other knights ate together. Pero Niño likewise took his place

at the dukes' table. This peace between the dukes
was but feigned, as was manifeſt thereafter, and
even that day he who would and could observe could
well underſtand that this kiss of peace was like that
which the traitor apoſtle gave to our Lord Jesus Chriſt.

[1406] When matters had been thus arranged
Pero Niño went a second time before the King's
Council, and said that the time was drawing near
when according to his plan which had sent him
thither, the galleys should set out again to make war
in England. He therefore demanded his wages that
he might pay his men. Forthwith they paid him the
money, though not all at once, nor all that was
owed him. Pero Niño left Paris and went to Rouen,
and paid and satisfied his men as beſt he might. Then
he went to see my lady of Serifontaine and her father,
my lord of Bellengues. There began to be some talk
of a marriage between Pero Niño and my lady; but
there were reasons on both sides why the marriage
should not be celebrated at once. One reason was
that the lady had been a widow but a short time,
and that being so great a lady and of such high eſtate,
she would not do an unseemly thing; the other reason
was that Pero Niño was setting out to the wars, and
moreover he muſt speak of this matter to his king and
obtain his leave before concluding anything. Therefore this time it remained agreed between them that
the lady should wait for two full years, so that Pero
Niño might have time to finish his business, both in

the war of which he had charge and with his lord the King. These matters thus resolved, they made each other presents of jewels, and Pero Niño having taken leave of the lady ſtarted for Rouen. At that place there came to him many knights and lords of Normandy to have speech with him concerning the war. And he left there with his galleys and came to the port of Harfleur. And as the galleys were leaving Rouen about the hour of prime and as they began to row, the sun was obscured, and all the men in the galleys and those on the shore were in great dread ; they told the captain that he should give up his departure, and that it was not a favourable omen for ſtarting on a campaign. The sailors were all agreed that they muſt not ſtart during all that moon. Some declared that the sun was wounded, which presaged a great mortality among mankind ; others said that there would be dreadful gales at sea, and many other things which each man said according to his underſtanding. Pero Niño thus answered them : " Friends, be not afraid ; there is no cause for fear. We are all Chriſtians, we believe in God and we worship Him. We should have no faith in omens ; have firm truſt in God who made all things, for He knows what He is doing. Which of us could penetrate His judgments and discern His designs ? He has not created us that we should judge His works, but that we should be humble and obedient to His commandments. Let us do what we have to do, and let Him do to us as shall seem good to Him. Let us call upon Him and ask His mercy, that He guide and guard us, and He will do it, for His word is truth. He hath said that He will be with us in our tribulations, and that if we call upon Him He will vouchsafe our prayers forthwith. If now it is dark, in a little time it will be light. But I would tell you what it is that causes an eclipse ; the sun is further from us than the moon, and it happens at this time that the moon is passing before the sun, and prevents the sunlight from reaching us ; for the moon herself is dark and has no other light but that which she receives from the sun, yet is formed of a body so subtle that when the sun shines upon her she receives its light which she transmits to us, the which is not hers but the sun's. The sun keeps all its light for ever ; it dies not, nor can it be wounded, nor be darker now than heretofore. It is no marvel that two men, one coming from China[115] and the other from Prussia, should cross the world and meet, and their meeting would give no cause for prophecy ; it would be a journey and not an omen. So do the sun and moon at this time ; they have met, and the moon has passed before the sun. The moon will continue her course, the sun its regular progress, and once more it will appear shining in splendour."

.   .   .

This saying of the captain pleased all his men mightily, and they loſt their fear. The sun shone again and lit up the world and Pero Niño ordered them to row on and to continue the voyage in the name of God.

While the captain was thus making his way up the Seine, the knights, gentlemen, ladies, and damsels who dwelt on the banks of the river came to see him and gave him great welcome. The galleys reached Harfleur ; there they found Messire Charles de Savoisy,

making ready his galleys to set out with the captain
Pero Niño. Three whalers of France well manned,
that the captain had engaged again, came thither to
put themselves under his orders, and they left Harfleur
altogether and went to the cape of la Hève.[116] They
took counsel together and agreed to enter the Flanders
Channel to seek for English ships. Coasting along
they passed the Cape of Caux which is where Normandy
marches with Picardy, and came to Boulogne and
Camiers[117] and to the cape of Sangate.[118] There begins
the country of Calais. The galleys entered the
Fosse-à-Cayeux,[119] and cast anchor before the town of
Le Crotoy which is in Picardy. It is a town of France
altogether surrounded by the sea : no man may reach
it from the land, except when the tide is low. The
galleys victualled there. All this harbour, at low tide,
is dry ; no more water is to be seen, and anyone who
should come from the land side during the six hours
of ebb, might well think that the sea never came there.
Over a great stretch of sand it seems no more wet than
as if it had been raining. Many men, beasts, and carts
come and go then from one land to the other. There
is a very deep moat before the town in which there is
water as if in a pool or lagoon, and therein do the ships
remain which cannot depart until the tide comes
back.

.   .   .

The captain and Messire Charles held a council,
and learnt that all the men on the coast of Cornwall
were kept on the watch, because of what the galleys
had done the year before in that land ; so they resolved
to get to the other coast of England, which is called the

North Sea Coaſt,[120] because the people of these parts were without diſtruſt, and they might be able to capture a few villages before the people had been warned. They set out from the port of Le Crotoy and entered the Flanders Channel, where they encountered very heavy weather. They hoiſted the ſtorm trysail and shipped the oars. The wind blew from the south-eaſt; the galleys had it aſtern, and running before it they passed between Calais and Dover, two English possessions. On the Flemish banks they had to face a violent gale. Such was the tempeſt that assailed the galleys on the prow that it washed on deck sand from the bottom of the sea mixed with the water. There are found there certain fishes which fly over the water; some passed flying above the galleys and others fell.[121] This sea is very perilous, and what they call the Flemish banks have received that name because the bottom of the sea is there like a number of ditches following one another. The sea makes and unmakes them, digging them out sometimes on one side and sometimes on the other. When they heave the lead there, in one place they find four or five fathoms, and in other places quite close a hundred or more. Because of this many vessels run aground there and are often loſt. The galleys passed before the watch tower, which is at the entry of Flanders, and ſteered for the North Sea coaſt, hoping to surprise a town which is called Orwell.[122] When they had made out this town, they remained at sea until night fell, so that they might not be sighted from the land. When night had fallen they held a council on board the captain's galley.

The town had a bridge which joined it to the other bank of the river, whence help might come ; for there were on the other side the bridge many towns well able to send help. The captain asked in the council that he might have the keeping of this bridge, for there should be great work there to defend it ; and moreover it was fitting that he should have this charge, for upon this defence hung all the success of the affair and the taking of the town. Some even said that Pero Niño wished to be dubbed knight that day and in that place, for he saw that it would be a day of great toil and peril. They resolved likewise that at break of day all should land and march upon the town ; and that night each busied himself to furnish himself with all things needful for the morrow.

All night long the wind blew from the south ; and at dawn it was so strong that the galleys were in great danger, for it blew from the sea and there was no shelter from it. It did not cease from worsening until the galleys were forced to draw off from the shore and to get back to the open sea. Thus were they prevented from landing at Orwell.

The galleys hugged the wind and sailed along all day. The wind was so furious that the galleys reached a point when they ran the risk of making land only in Prussia or in Scotland ; they would then have had to sail at the leaſt for four or five hundred leagues. However, by dint of great exertions, for the wind carried them before it, and with the help of God, they contrived to reach the watch tower and to enter into the port of Flanders. By this port there is a town which is called Sluys. The captain was very well received there, and the people of the country rejoiced much to see him, the more that at this time the rumour ran that the English fleet was coming. Thence the captain went to visit the city of Bruges, which is six leagues off.[123] There were at Bruges many merchants of Castille who paid him much honour and many services.

The captain bought there cloth, arms, and jewels and came back to Sluys. In the meanwhile there came up four ships of Portugal, and Messire Charles asked the captain to aid him in their capture, which might fairly be made, because the Portuguese were enemies of France and used to bear aid to the English. But the Portuguese commended themselves to the captain, imploring his mercy to protect them against Messire Charles. And the captain asked Messire Charles for the love he bore him to let them go, for there was at that time truce between Castille and Portugal, and Messire Charles let them go this time, but much against his will.

The captain and Messire Charles left Sluys and turned back into the Flanders Channel, and passed before Calais, a town of the English domain, which is in the Flemish country.[124] Calais is a town set on a plain ; and when the tide makes it reaches right up to the city and even surrounds it, though at low tide they can enter it from the land. It is all surrounded by French lands. They said that it was then thirty years since the English had stolen it from France,[125] that had used to hold it. The city had a very ſtrong wall, well furnished with towers, with a moat full of water that was crossed by a draw-bridge. The captain wished to go up to the town and capture some vessels, had not the tide been ebbing, and had they not fired at him from the town very powerful bombards which carried far out to sea. That night the galleys reached a harbour which is called Nuleta,[126] in France. There was there a garrison of men at arms and archers, who had for captain a brave Caſtillian man at arms named Ochoa Barva.

The next morning, the galleys and the whalers set sail to cross over to England, and looking seawards sighted a fleet of ships spread out in a circle, for it was a calm. The galleys and the whalers saw that it was the English fleet, and that there were in it great sailing ships and whalers, all manned for war. The captain ordered a ſtandard to be hoiſted, as is the cuſtom at sea to summon a council; and he said to Messire Charles: "There are the English, and the sea is calm; let us go againſt them." Messire Charles answered: "My lord, there are there many vessels, and among them great ships; they are far off from the land, and if a wind rises, which cannot be long tarrying on this sea, we should find ourselves in great jeopardy among them." The captain replied: "At present the sea is calm, and there is no wind; while the calm laſts and while we have ſtill time let us do our duty. When the wind shall arise, let us do as circumſtances require. Well know ye what harm has been done you by the English, and how much havoc they make every day in Caſtille and in France. If now we let them go,

never again shall we have such a chance to fight them.
And what will be worse, if we let them go, they will
see that we do it from fear, and henceforward they
will do yet more harm to us, for they will go about it
with less fear. If I could have believed that we ought
to let them go, never would I have come to France
and never made acquaintance with the French."
Messire Charles, when he perceived the will of the
captain, said : " Let us do as you shall command."

Thereupon the captain gave orders to his galleys
as to what they should do ; and, encouraging his men,
he bade them pass wine down the oarsmen's gangway ;
for on such occasions it is needful and most profitable,
for on the galleys men abstain from wine, and when
they drink it drink little. Taken thus, wine does much
good and gives heart and gaiety to him who drinks it.
It is of this wine that the prophet speaks, when he
says : " Wine rejoices the heart of men, and bread
strengthens it." He says it not for those who drink
to excess, and lose judgment, and sink into baseness
and infamy. Of these last has the philosopher said :
" Wine is a seducing demon, which, little by little,
by its savour, brings men under its yoke." The
captain ordered them to arm on the upper deck.
Meanwhile the English did not remain idle. They
crowded on sail, drew up their great whalers in line.
and set in the rear two great sailing ships and a German
vessel, with the small whalers in the middle. So they
arranged the sailing boats, and they had further some
whalers with oars and with sails. Then they hoisted
their flags at the poop.

The whalers are long and low in the side. Fair

PLATE VI

THE FLEET

troops and men at arms appeared, well armed with
lances, and bows and arrows. The captain's galleys
and the whalers went towards them and opened a
fierce conflict of arrows, darts, bolts and ſtones. The
captain had quarrells dressed with tar with which he
burned the sails of the English. Soon he ordered us
to push forward to board them ; but all did not fight
with the same heart. Then he bade us set fire to
a long-boat full of tar, and to send it into the midſt
of the English whalers to fire them ; for they were all
pressed close one againſt the other. The captain's
galley advanced, pushing forward this long boat with
a spar, and the English thruſt it aside with their lances.
While the captain was ſtriving to faſten the fire-ship
upon them, and at the same time fighting fiercely,
the sea wind arose behind the English, and began to
serve the sails of their ships ; but such was the fury
of the fight that no one on the captain's galley perceived
it, whilſt all the reſt were aware of it. Messire
Charles gave up the battle and let the prows of his
ships veer with the wind. They warned the captain,
and shewed him how the great English sailing ships
had caught the wind and were coming upon him, and
that he would do well to leave the battle and to work
his ship to get out of it. The captain did not believe
what they told him but thought that they spoke thus
so that they should not have to fight ; and he said :
" Let him who is afraid take to flight ; but this time
either they shall carry us away prisoners to England,
or we will take them to France, or he shall die whom
God wills to die." The sailors, seeing how great
was the danger, and that all the other galleys were

rowing away ſtriving with each other who could row faſteſt, changed the galley's course without the captain's sight or knowledge. When he saw that his galley was out of the enemy's reach, he demanded why they had done this, and how they had dared to do it. The sailors answered : " My lord, see how all the galleys have left you, as well your own as those of France, and see how the English ships have a favourable wind, and are all coming againſt us." The good knight looked, and said : " May God's will be done ; and since it has so fallen out, and that luck has turned, do the reſt of you do as you think ought now to be done."

All the English ships came up againſt the captain, and took no heed of any other galley but h⁙s ; they could not reach the others that had caught the wind, and already the great sailing ships were very close to the captain, making ready to attack him. Well do I believe that his other galleys, seeing him in such a plight, muſt have thought that the captain would be killed or taken prisoner. His galley was between two whalers, fighting with them both ; and if the whalers had dared approach the galley they could have held her until the ſtronger vessels had come up. Meanwhile, the whalers of France were sailing how and where they would, for they were faſt clippers ; and one of them which was at the head of the line, seeing that the galley of the captain was running great risks, for she was already surrounded by the English and the two whalers were making ready to bar her course, did a fair feat of seamanship. They luffed and shook her, letting the wind ſtrike the yards by the head ;

and she awaited the English, so that the captain and
his men thought that she had broken some of her
rigging and could make no way. The captain gave
orders that they should make for her and succour her,
for she lay in the midſt of the English ships. Then
did the whaler ſtrike a fair blow. So soon as they saw
that the English were to leeward of them,[127] they set
their sail so that they scudded before the wind, and
passed between them very swiftly, paying no more heed
to them all than does a swift courser manœuvring
between great and heavy horses. And although she
was of ordinary size, the whaler ran againſt one of
the whalers which were pursuing the captain's galley,
took her on the beam near the prow, broke her
bowsprit, cut her ſtay, and altogether disabled her.
Well do I believe that she killed men aboard the
English ship in this ramming ; and her crew would have
taken her, but that they did not dare caſt the grappling
irons on her, since they were in the midſt of the
English ; but rather let her float off, and themselves
got into safety. This was done in such wise that
not a single whaler dared to come near them by herself,
but all sought together to ſtop them so that they got
out from among them keeping them off with boat
hooks.[128] As for the captain's galley, she would have
been boarded by the English whalers, if we had not
fought as she went, vigorously defending ourselves with
bolts and with flights of arrows and darts.

The galleys during this time had drawn in close to
the coaſt of France, and the wind dropped a little.
Then his other galleys and his whaling boats rallied
to the captain ; and when he had them once more

together, he bade them await the English there and fight them. But the English did not dare come. And the captain had signals made to them to provoke them to a fight. I think they came not because they did not dare fteer their sailing ships and their hulks where the galleys were, and also that the wind was light near the coaft.

. . .

The captain railed againft wind and fortune, for he would have captured all this fleet of English, had the wind risen an hour later. The King of England had manned the fleet; he was sending with it one of his daughters[129] who was going to wed the Duke of Holland, and with her were many great lords, great ladies, women and maidens, and much riches. The captain had then good reason for lamentation.

After this adventure the galleys came before a town of France that is called Gravelines.[130] There was there a garrison of Caftillians in the pay of the King of France, and they had seen the fight from the shore and what had passed between them and the English. They came to pay their respects to the captain, telling him that they wished they had been with him to second him. The galleys and whaling boats left there, and, keeping along the coaft of Picardy, entered the harbour of Le Crotoy. There they refted, made provision of water, biscuit, and other things of which they had need, and then resolved to cross to England. But weather and fortune willed that they should ftay

a month in this port, without ever being able to leave
it. Every time that they ſtrove to reach the sea they
found the weather adverse and the wind blowing into
the middle of the harbour. The men of the galleys
there spent all of their resources that remained, for it
was already two years since they had left Caſtille ;
but this diſtrict profited much by their presence, for
so long as the captain was there never did the English
ships appear who were wont to come every year to
ravage that country.

Messire Charles had already spent all his money,
and was not able any longer to pay his men, and they
all left him, so that it was impossible for him to set
out with the captain. One day when the wind fell,
Pero Niño took leave of the knights of those parts and
of Messire Charles. The good knight was much vexed
that he could not bear him company, and Pero Niño
that he could not help in such a need. Pero Niño
left the port with the whalers that had come from
France with him, and passed the Fosse-à-Cayeux,
making for Normandy. One morning at dawn, six
whaling boats well manned appeared round the Cape
of Caux, having a fair wind in their sails. They were
coming out of Harfleur when the galleys sighted them.
They hugged the shore, thinking that these were
English vessels, and hoping that as the wind dropped
they might get up with them. The captain, againſt
the counsel of his sailors, ordered that they should
draw near to see what manner of men they were.
They, sighting the galleys, furled their sails, hoiſted
the flag of France, and saluted, which shewed that
they were French. The captain returned their

salute ; then they drew near, paid their respects to the captain, and spoke with him ; and all were friends or acquaintances. They told him that they were going out at random to seek for English ships, and that if their company was agreeable to him he had only to shew the way and they would all follow. Pero Niño rejoiced greatly at this meeting, and it was decided among them to steer for the coast of Brittany to see if they could find any English ships. One day at dawn as many as a hundred and twenty sails appeared off the Brittany coast. The galleys sped towards them, thinking to have to do with the English and to reach them easily, for the sea was calm and these ships had little wind in their sails. But it happened that they were French, going to load up with salt in a port of Brittany which is called the port of Batz.[131] The captain held counsel with the shipmasters and with Guillaume and Jacques Bouxières,[132] who were the masters of the whalers, proposing to them to cross to England, but the Normans said to him : " My lord, there is quite near here a very rich English island, called Jersey[133] the Great ; and if you could have sufficient men to land there and fight against four or five thousand men who dwell there, it would be great honour to you to vanquish them ; and moreover you might gain great ransom therefrom." They said further : " You have now great renown as a good knight and a good warrior. Near here is Brittany ; approach the coast, and send your letters to the lords of these parts who are in the neighbourhood and ask them to come to see you ; all will come at your request, and you can speak with them. Meanwhile

keep these ships here, that were going for salt."
Accordingly the captain asked the men in the ships to
stay, for matters that concerned the service of their
lord the King of France, and to accompany him to the
island of Jersey, where they would have their share
alike in the honour and the profit that might be found
there. They answered that at his prayer and request
they would do what they would not have done for any
knight of France who might have asked for it. Then
there came to the coast, where the captain had
anchored, a multitude of folk, amongst whom were
good knights, men at arms and archers. The captain
said to them : " My lords, knights and gentlemen,
well know ye that I am sent by my lord the king of
Castille, to help the Crown of France, and to make
war against the English ; and likewise, how last year
I crossed to England, and how it pleased God to give
me and mine victory over the English, in several
places where we went to fight them, and where they
were defeated and had ever the worst of it. I have
scoured all the coast of Cornwall and a part of that
of the North Sea ; and now I perceive that all these
folk are watchful and gathered together to defend
their country, so that a great fleet and a multitude
of men are needed if a landing is to be made and a
foothold held. The sailing ships which, as you all
know, the king sent thither from Castille, will not
help me ; and for myself I have only these three
galleys, and these noble folk of Normandy, whom it
pleases to second me, and who come in my company to
serve the King of France. Knights and gentlemen
here present, let us, I pray you, join forces ; and we

will cross to the island of Jersey, and we may have a good day's work with the knights and the folk that are in that island." There was there among the Bretons Hector de Pontbriant and the lord of Tournemine[134]; and the Bretons answered: "My lord captain, you are most welcome in these parts; for we all, knights of this country, were wishful to see you, having heard very good report of you, and that you are a good and gallant knight. We give you many thanks that you have taken upon yourself the burden of such an enterprise, for the which we will give you aid and go with you most willingly; and you shall command us, and we will obey you as if you were our own natural lord, in this affair and in any other that you like to begin; for we think that with your courage and good luck we shall be victors and shall gain honour and renown wheresoever we may be with you." The captain answered: "My lords, the courage and the valour are on your side; as for me, with the help of God and of our Lady St Mary, I will do what I can, and I have trust in God that victory and honour shall be ours." The captain added: "I would have wished to cross to England, but it is too late, for already the winter is here; and were we to have vessels manned on purpose it might be too late. But you well know the great island of Jersey, that it is only seven sea leagues hence; we may be there quickly, and together fight against four or five thousand men fit to bear arms who live there, if you are agreed to go to the island." All answered that it would be well, and went forthwith to prepare themselves.

In two days' time they took to sea well prepared.

They set out rowing and sailing; the weather was good, and they reached the island. The men of the island, when they saw the fleet in the harbour, gathered together in hafte and came in great numbers to the shore. That very night forty or fifty men of little wit, without orders from the captain, landed to colleƈt shell-fish, and began to skirmish with the inhabitants of the island; and thus skirmishing, the seamen fled towards the sea, and the English behind them. They were at once succoured and picked up by the ships. This gave great pride and confidence to the English, which served them ill the next day, as you shall see. In the evening the captain had the knights and other men assembled, and treated them to rough words, telling them that because of the like disorder that there was among them they would often be beaten and discomfited; that he besought them to behave better for the future, and that each should for himself and his men put his affairs in such order that no ill or harm should befall; otherwise he would be forced to make an example and to impose punishments. Thereupon he had it cried that none should dare to go ashore nor get into the cutters without his orders, nor leave the fleet under pain of death; and further, that no one should begin any fight whatsoever or depart from his hoft, unless the trumpets sounded and the captain's banner went forward.

Near the great island of Jersey there is another little island in which is a hermitage to St Mary, and the captain ordered that all the men of his fleet should land on this island arrayed for battle. When the tide is high, the water divides this little island from the greater, and none can cross from one to the other except in a boat ; but when the tide is low a man can cross dryshod. It is a very secure place to put a gangway ashore and make a shelter where a few men may easily defend themselves againſt many.

The captain Pero Niño, the other knights, and all the reſt of the soldiers landed there during the night, and the knights asked Pero Niño to array the hoſt as he would and to dispose all things as he might judge needful for the morrow, and that all would be under his command and at his orders. And the captain said : " Sirs, here are you, good knights, skilled in war. You have been in other great exploits of war ; array yourselves as you consider fitting." But they insiſted that he should take command. The captain said that it was a very heavy charge for a single man, especially on foot, but that he would undertake it with a good will. Then the captain unfolded to them what they had to do, and how they muſt set about it. He chose out those who were to remain in the ships, and ordered the fashion in which the hoſts should be drawn up, and the pavisade, and the crossbowmen, and the archers ; and, how, if they won the day, they were to advance warily, in case there were ambuscades, and all the other matters which have to be foreseen on such occasions.

As soon as everything was settled, the captain ordered all the galleys and all the ships to draw away from the land and to go out to sea, so that his men should not think they could save themselves by flight, if any mishap befell. He only kept near the land three boats of his own, in which were good crossbowmen, with the order that if any of the men of the French and Castillian ships came towards the sea in flight, they were to shoot at them with their cross-bows and kill them. Then he bade them spend the rest of the night in eating and in sleeping a little, in such wise that two hours before dawn everyone should be armed and ready for battle. He set a guard to watch the passage between the little island and the greater, for fear that the English might seize it when the tide should fall.

On the morrow, at break of day, everyone was up and ready. The tide was low. The trumpets sounded and they crossed over to the large island. Pero Niño set the men at arms in array according as it had been decided; he posted each man in the place where he should be, set his standard in the midst of them, and said to them: " Keep in the array in which I have set you, while I go to array the rest of my men. Let me have the archers and the soldier's boys,[135] and I will set them where they can fight best and have the most cover; and when I have posted them as they ought to be, I will come back to you. Meanwhile keep quiet, and let no one budge from the place where I leave him." The Bretons told him that in the name of God they would do what he thought best. The captain gathered together all his archers and crossbowmen and his own men; he made two pavisades, each of sixty great shields, divided into two parts after the manner of wings, and he posted the archers and crossbowmen behind them. He gave them a standard of his arms which a brave man at arms of his bore; he put with them the soldiers' boys and those who were ill armed and to encourage them said : " Now, my friends, you see how you are in the enemy's country. Look, there they are drawn up for battle, well armed and ready to come against us, just as we are to march against them. They are many, but they are neither so brave nor so strong as you. Look at the sea, you have it behind you ; and as there is no one left in the ships, do not put your trust in them. See how you are betwixt two enemies, sea and land. Fight hard, do not let yourselves be beaten ; be all firm and single-hearted, for you cannot escape by flight, you would all perish in the sea. Moreover, if you let yourselves be taken prisoners, you know how the English treat the Castillians, and how they are piti-less enemies. If you stand firm and fight well, you will have honour and much good booty. Look how rich and fair is this country ! All that you see shall be yours if only you fight well. Make ready, and act like men of courage. Take good heed ! let no man leave his place where I have set him : do not budge until the enemy have come to you. Call all upon St James, who is our patron of Spain, that he may help us."

The captain went away and left them thirty or forty paces forward, and came back to the men at arms. The knights formed a host in good array in the order in which the captain had left them, their ensigns[136] close by the captain's banner, and under the banner as many men as could stand there. There were there both Normans and Bretons, and there may have been

in that hoſt of the captain's as many as a thousand
men at arms, Caſtillians, Bretons and Normans.
You can underſtand what a task it was for a single
knight to array and command so many men, and he
fully armed except for the head. There was not a
single man at arms or foot soldier whom he did not
touch to array him, speaking to each two or three
times and telling him what he had to do.

The English, likewise, had their men well arrayed
in hoſts ; there may have been three thousand men
on foot, and up to two hundred on horseback. These
latter came forward along the shore under the command of a knight of England, hoping to outflank our
men ; but the captain looked to it by turning some to
face them, and they had such a reception that they
had to withdraw. The English then began to move,
and when they had come near, Pero Niño had the
trumpets sounded ; then the hoſts advanced a little,
marching slowly, and then he ordered them to ſtop.
At this moment the English came againſt the hoſts
very ſturdily, and attacked vigorously. They charged
all together, except for a great hoſt where there were
at leaſt a thousand men at arms who came behind on
foot well in line. Those in the van were, on the other
hand, in great disorder, and came very proudly to
ſtrike hard againſt the pavisades. The Caſtillians
gave them a warm welcome with ſtones, and darts, and
lances, and shafts, and arrows, so that in this firſt
encounter many killed and wounded fell on the English
side. However, the English obſtinately ſtrove to
carry the position ; but the Caſtillians defended it
ſteadfaſtly and fought so vigorously that every moment

it went worse with the English, so that in the end, much against their will, they shewed their heels. Then the English men at arms advanced ; and as the men with the pavisades and the crossbowmen were already scattered in pursuit of the others who were fleeing, these men at arms came through the middle of the line and reached the captain's hoſt, and the captain had them march againſt them. There were ſtruck very fair blows with the lance wherewith many were hit on both sides and some even overthrown. Leaving the lances they grasped axes and swords and engaged in a rough mellay. There might you have seen helmets torn from breaſtplates, and arm and leg pieces ſtripped off from some, and axes and swords fall from the hands of others ; some come to grips one with the other or take to their daggers ; some fall to the ground, others rise again, and blood flowing abundantly in many places.[137] The conflict was so desperate and the press such that even he who came out of it beſt had none the less hard enough toil. So brave were they on both sides, and so much obſtinacy did they bring to it, that without a good discovery of Pero Niño's, in a few hours they would all have killed each other, or only a very few would have been left alive. Pero Niño looked and saw a white flag with the cross of St George which was kept upright, though many ſtandards had been beaten down ; he called the good knight Hector de Pontbriant and a few of his men at arms, those whom he knew, and the Normans who ſtill surrounded him, and said to them : " Friends, so long as this flag flies, these English will never allow themselves to be beaten ; let us do all we can to take it." Then the captain and Hector de Pontbriant with about fifty men at arms came out of the hoſt and, wheeling swiftly beyond the hoſts, reached the place where the banner ſtood. They had to fight very hard with those who were there, for they were very good knights; but in the firſt encounter our men slew their captain; they called him the Receiver-General, and I saw him lying at my feet. He was dying, and they could not bear him away, so close was the press of combatants. There died with him other Englishmen, and the colour was beaten down. When the English saw that matters were going so ill for them, they began to fly, each whither he could. To all this can teſtify he who bore the captain's banner, and they who bore the other ſtandards, since they could not fight but could only look on and ſtay firm at their poſts. The English ran, throwing off helmets, armour and leather jerkins to fly the better; and the Caſtillians and the French were so weary and so many of them wounded that they could not pursue them.

The place where this battle was fought was a great shore of sand which ſtretched for half a league; it was scattered with jerkins,[138] arms and shields[139] which those who fled had thrown away. Then the rowers, the soldiers' boys and the crossbowmen ran scattered over the country, plundering and burning without fear. Before the battle the captain had ordered that if it befell that they won the day and discomfited the English, the hoſt of the men at arms should at once form up again, for fear that there might be an ambuscade, or that more folk should come up and find our men in disorder. Pero Niño had more trouble now than he had had in the beginning to array the ranks; none the less he went on until in the end all the men at arms were gathered together. And the captain ordered Gutierre Diez de Gamez, his ſtandard bearer, to ſtay at his poſt with the banner in the midſt of the hoſt, while he himself and a few knights went to pick up those of their men who were scattered over the countryside in bad array. And the captain went with about fifty knights, mounted on horses they had taken in the battle.

The country was close set with great woods, cut up with gardens and hedges of trees, and they went down the valleys, and could not be seen. The hoſt of the men at arms ſtayed poſted until the captain came back with his men, which was a good two hours. The captain then ordered everyone back to the galleys and the hoſt of the men at arms ſtayed where they were until all the reſt had gone aboard. Pero Niño had left men to guard the little island and to make ready food for all that should wish to eat. He crossed to the island with his men at arms, and the knights and many of the gentlemen supped with him there, and then they tended the wounded. Afterwards the captain had the prisoners brought before him, and queſtioned them concerning the country, what men were in the island and what fortresses, how many and who guarded them, and if they knew where was the English fleet and how many manned ships did they say it was reckoned at. Those of the prisoners who were the beſt informed answered that there were in the island five fortified caſtles well furnished, which knights of England guarded, that the inhabitants of

the island might be four or five thousand men, and
that there was a captain who came from England
whom the king had sent to govern them; that
he had come with them to the battle, and that they
did not know if he were dead; that the other people,
burgesses, labourers, and fishermen, were within a
town, the greatest in the island, enclosed with pali-
sades and good moats filled with water, wherein
they had their goods, their wives and their children,
and that the moſt part of those who had escaped from
the battle had retreated thither; but that they had
always kept a law and ordinance that, if anyone wished
to seize their city, they must all die before they
suffered it. Pero Niño thus came to know how matters
were in the island. They told him further that the
English fleet was at Plymouth,[140] and that it was of
two hundred sail, among which were Caſtillian ships,
hulks, boats and whalers all well manned, that they
were expecting them from day to day, and that their
coming was delayed only by the contrary wind.

Thereupon the captain held a council with the
knights, and all agreed with him in the opinion that
on the morrow they muſt, if they could, take that city
and fire the whole country. The captain said:
" Sirs, thanks be to God, we have beaten these folk
in battle; in case they come once more againſt us,
we shall easily beat them again. It appears to me
that it would be better for us to make ourselves
maſters of this island and to keep it for ourselves,
rather than burn the country. Let us send to tell the
inhabitants that they are to come to submit themselves and to do homage and that otherwise we will

destroy them and their country; then we shall see what they mean to do."

The Bretons answered: " My lord, unless we get the castles into our power, we cannot make ourselves masters in the land; but if you would order it, my lord, we will burn, sack, and get away hence." Pero Niño replied: " Let us go towards the city, and see if they want to fight; when we are there, if they do not come forth, we will hold another council." They agreed that the captain had spoken well and that they would do as he ordered. That night Pero Niño commanded that early on the morrow they should all be ready to assault the city; he set guards over the passage to the little island, and all slept and rested. At dawn the trumpets sounded; the captain's banner went forward, and all with it. That day the captain was able to command everyone more easily and with less weariness, for he had with him good knights, and more than a hundred were mounted on horses that they had captured in the battle and taken in the country. The captain formed a vanguard and rear-guard for the march, for it was two leagues to the city, and he sent forward light-armed men to fire the country. The countryside was covered with houses, gardens, crops and herds; and all the country burned, which was a very piteous thing to see, for the folk who lived there were Christians. They were marching thus when there came to us an English gentleman in the garb of a herald, asking for the captain of Spain, since all those in the island knew of everything that was happening on our side, being informed by a man they had captured in the first skirmish when our men were few and had allowed themselves beaten. They brought him to the captain Pero Niño. He knelt before him and said: "Mi ye rragotth geuogoth endachà,"[141] which means: "God save you and give you good days." "The people of this country commend themselves to your mercy and send to beseech you for the love of God to have pity upon them, for you should have had your fill. You have come to seek them out in their own land; you have beaten them in battle; you have wounded, killed and captured a great number of their men; you have ravaged their country; and now it appears that you wish to go and make an end of them. They ask you for the love of God and of your pity not to do so, for they are Catholic Christians, and are in no wise contrary to the faith of Jesus Christ, and do not deserve extermination at your hands. Further, for the love of the Queen of Castille, who was born in the kingdom of England, who is your lady, who, ye know well, would not rejoice at all this ill, have mercy upon them."

When the Englishman had finished his discourse, the captain made answer and said: "Go back to those who sent you; tell them to send to me four or five men of the best among them with whom I may speak. I will warrant their coming and going, that they shall suffer no harm." The Englishman departed, and five honourable men of the city came to the captain and kissed his hand, and he said to them: "I have heard the grievances that you bring against me. You well know, all of you, that the English fleet, when it comes to make war against Spain, first comes here and furnishes itself with victuals and men; wherefore both you and they are enemies of Castille. Moreover these islands pertain to Brittany; you were beforetime Bretons, and by the wickedness of those whose descendants you are, you revolted and made yourselves English. Thus it behoves you to recognise me as your lord and to submit yourselves to me, in the name of my lord the king of Castille; otherwise I tell you that all shall be put to fire and sword, both you and your country."

They answered: "True it is, my lord, that these four islands used to belong to Brittany, and that we are of Breton race; but the English conquered this country of old, as often happens, in many places, that men are made subject to their enemies and constrained to serve those who please them not, not by love, but by fear, and more by force than willingly. Our fathers have left us in this servitude. We cannot free ourselves from the English, unless others who are stronger take us from them, for the fortresses of this country are all held by English knights; and my lord, if you could get the castles, we would do your will. Otherwise what we might do would be of little worth; you could not defend us, and you would leave us in great jeopardy at the hands of the English. What we can do, that ask, and we will do it."

The captain answered: "As for the castles, I have trust in God to conquer them speedily; meanwhile give up to me the city that you dwell in." They said: "My lord, we will go back thither and return with an answer." They departed, and thereupon we came near the city, about half a league off. The captain, while he awaited their return, ſtayed his troops, ordering them not to go beyond the creſt of a hill whence the people of the city could see our men drawn up in a hoſt very near them.

The English came back to the captain and said : " My lord, the folk of the city commend themselves to your mercy, and send to tell you that the city and the caſtle is all they have, and that they have always had it, and that never have French or English entered therein, and that they have always held it thus up to the present by privilege, that they and their goods might be the better guarded, and that they have a law never to deliver it up either to enemies or to friends, and that before they let it be taken by force they are all to die, because there are their wives, their children and their goods ; if you ask of them gold and silver, ſtuffs and other things, they will give you what they can gather together ; but do them no more ill and harm. Let it please you then not to come to their city, for it might hap that you should take it : but be assured that it would firſt coſt the life of more than one man you love, and that you would have to kill men, women and children, all that you should find in the city, and that this would be so heavy a burden upon your conscience that never would God give you pardon."

Then Pero Niño held his council, to ask what should be done, and they said to him : " My lord, these men give very good reasons and their pleas are juſt ; it is reasonable that you should concede and grant what they ask. You have not now time to ſtay here for several reasons " (which they adduced). Others at the same time laid stress on their saying that they were willing to buy themselves off with a ransom ; and mediators proposed that they should give the captain ten thousand golden crowns, and that he should leave them in peace. The captain, for the love of God, answered that it would please him to have pity upon them, and that they might therefore give these ten thousand crowns in gold, so that they could be shared out among the soldiers. Many reasons drove him to conclude this treaty. There was great danger for our men, for they were very far from their ships ; and further, men should not press every affair with such obstinacy, for in the end thereof they may sometimes fall into greater evil.

.   .   .

But all such things fall out as time permits ; and Pero Niño acted according to his time and strength. He said further to the men of the city : " You shall give me every year for ten years, counting from to-day, twelve lances, twelve axes, twelve bows with their arrows, and twelve trumpets." This it cost them much to accord ; but they agreed to do so, and so it was decreed. Forthwith they handed over a part of the crowns of their ransom ; for the rest that remained to be paid they delivered up four men, the richest in the country, as sureties, and Pero Niño carried them away with him. When all this was finished, the trumpets sounded, the banner and his troops, all well arrayed, returned to the harbour where were the ships, and he ordered all to assemble by the sea. Meanwhile the people belonging to the salt-ships had taken to the sea-shore flocks, horses, mares, cows, and great booty taken from the houses; they loaded everything into their ships, Pero Niño took his leave of them, and they continued their voyage. The captain Pero Niño asked the Breton and Norman knights all to come with him to the port of Breſt, where there is a good town of Brittany. That day when they embarked to leave the island, horses were cheap; they sold a horse for five or six half-sols, which makes ten maravedis. All came to Breſt, as the captain had asked. They were well received there, and great rejoicings were made at their coming, for that they had carried the day in the battle. The captain feaſted them for the time that they remained there. Merchants of Brittany came to the captain, and he handed over to them the hoſtages of the island; and they gave him what remained unpaid of the ten thousand crowns which were to be the price of the ransom. The captain divided this money very fairly between the Bretons, the Normans, and his own men at arms, to each man according to his rank. Then they parted and each went his way.

Pero Niño sent a messenger to Paris to take his leave of the King and the Dukes, for his lord the King had sent to bid him return to Caſtille. The galleys left Breſt and came to St Malo.[142] They then crossed the St Malo Race. They were already at the beginning of winter, in the month of October: that day the wind was from the North Eaſt,[143] which is very ſtrong at that season. They hoiſted the trysails and shipped the oars; the wind was aſtern, and the galleys profited

by the ebb to go out with the tide. As they were
sailing thus, the time came for the tide to turn, and
the tide began to make, and the galleys were ſtill in
the middle of the Race. The current of the rising
tide was ſtrong and caught the galleys at the prow ;
the wind was very ſtrong aſtern and fought againſt the
current at the prow. The galleys could make no
headway : the wind which was violent would not let
them go back, and the current, no less ſtrong, prevented them from going forward. All the sails were
spread, the sheets slacked. The great waves beat at
the prow, so that the galleys were in great diſtress
and danger. In the Race the water is all in whirlpools, and for this reason the sea is there more perilous.
The galleys ſtrove thus for six hours until the ebb
came. The wind freshened more and more ; it tore
the captain's sail and broke the lateen-yard, and the
current dragged the galley sideways ; and if the
auxiliary rudders had come unfixed at that moment,
the galley would have gone down. But there were at
the helms men ſtrong and skilled, who maſtered them
by great force. When they found themselves in
such a pass, they unshipped the oars with all speed.
Already the current was changing with the falling
tide ; they hoiſted the great sail, and with the wind
aſtern made headway. And even as the captain's
galley was in danger in the Race, so were all the others,
and some more. The galleys got out thence, and
came to the island of Batz. Thus coaſting along the
Brittany coaſt, sometimes with a fair wind, sometimes in heavy weather, they reached shelter near the
land, and passed the night there.

The Weſtern sea is not like the Mediterranean, which has neither ebb nor flow nor great currents, if one excepts one which is called the Faro current,[144] which is very dangerous, and wherein many vessels have perished. When the wind is against the current, the vessel which is between the two comes very close to death. In the Mediterranean there are many shoals; but if a galley wants to anchor for the night, she has only to find a rock to shelter her from the wind, she can be there without fear of the sea. Otherwise winds are not worse upon the one than the other; there are calms which may laſt several hours or even days. The Weſtern sea is moſt evil, especially for galleys. On the coaſts of both France and England there are neither creeks, nor good havens, because if it happen that the galley has anchored by the land in a spot where it may be sheltered from sea and wind, soon the tide falls, and unless they take heed they find themselves high and dry. Then they have to haſten to weigh anchor and to seek a better shelter in time, or take to the open sea, which is dangerous for galleys, for the calm never laſts long there. For galleys, if it were possible, it would be beſt never to have wind at all.

And thus it befell the captain's galleys, which had to endure a great tempeſt all day and part of the night. They went to the coaſt of Brittany, near mount St Michael, to seek a haven where the crew, who were very weary, might reſt. At midnight, they caſt anchor; and when day broke, rocks showed above the water all round the galleys. The sailors made soundings, and found that they were nearly aground

on a rocky bottom, which is very dangerous. Then all
the skill of the sailors was needed, for the wind blew
from the main and ſtruck the ships sideways; and as
the tide fell there was no hope that it would get them
out. The captain ordered all his men to jump into
the sea, to lighten the galleys, and to bear them along
by main force. And it pleased God that they should
succeed in getting out; they pushed the ships into
deep water and got them out of this evil place where
they were already ſtranded. Then everyone got back
on board the galleys, and they took to their oars, and
crossed the Race of Blanchart, and ſteered for the
cape of St Matthew. At this cape the two seas
meet, the Weſtern sea and the sea of Spain.[145] The
waves were very high there and the ſtorm so great
that the seas broke in the middle of the galleys.
Everyone was sent below, and the hatches battened
down. Then in the fear of death, the men made
vows and promises, some to St Mary of Guadalupe,
some to St James of Galicia, some to St Mary of
Finiſterre, some to Brother Pero Gonzalez of Tuy,
others to St Vincent of the Cape; and it pleased God
to hear them. The cape was rounded; and on the
other side they found the sea quiet and the wind less
ſtrong; and coaſting along the islands of Brittany,
they ſteered for La Rochelle.

.   .   .

After he had come out of the Flanders Channel, the
captain Pero Niño made his way to La Rochelle with
his galleys, and there refurnished them with everything that they had loſt at sea, and during the gales.
They took in water and victuals, and the captain

ordered them to set their course for Spain. When
the galleys left La Rochelle the wind blew from the
weſt, and when they were out at sea it veered to the
south weſt and blew with such violence that it forced
them towards the coaſt of the Maransin[146], which
is between Bordeaux and Bayonne, a moſt perilous
coaſt where there is neither harbour nor creek, nor
shelter of any sort, but only great rocks and shoals
ſtretching far out to sea, where perish the ships that
ſtrike them. But it pleased God that the south-weſt
wind should drop, and the galleys which had been
scattered by the ſtorm, came up again to the captain's
galley by ſteering for his ship's lantern, for it was
night. Messire Robin de Braquemont, a great French
knight, and the Bishop of Saint Flour,[147] who were
going as ambassadors of France to Spain, and were
each aboard a great sailing ship, found themselves
in this same evil pass. At midnight they drew near
the captain's galley, beseeching the favour that he
would not draw off far from them all that night, for
they were in great dread of sinking off the coaſt of
the Maransin, because the wind was always driving
them in shore, and they feared if the wind increased,
that they would be in great danger. The captain
remained all night on the watch, and at dawn the wind
fell. The captain then had a ſtandard hoiſted, and all
the ships rallied round his galley : they might then have
been in the middle of the Spanish sea. Messire
Robin and the Bishop came over to the captain's
galley and ate with him, while their ships ſtruck sail.
They had not yet finished eating when a very ſtrong
wind rose from the weſt, and raised the sea in a manner

that boded no good. The captain saw that it was a gale, and would not allow the ambassadors to go back on board their ships, but gave the ships the order to continue on their course. All that day the wind blew very fresh on the prow, and the galleys by dint of rowing reached land on the coaſt of Spain. As night fell they anchored in sixty fathoms, and spent the night in backing up their anchors and renewing their cables, for the strong wind made them drag their anchors. When the day dawned the tide rose and the galleys entered El Pasage, which is a harbour of Caſtille, sheltered from all the winds. During all this time the two sailing ships did not appear, however far out they watched the sea ; but at laſt, on the third day, they were sighted. Then the captain ordered their course to be set for Santander, and thither came the sailing vessels much battered by the foul weather that they had gone through. Pero Niño and the Ambassadors landed at Santander, and he was very well received and found there a King's messenger with a letter in which the king bade him come to him forthwith, for as soon as the captain was off the coaſt of Spain the King knew of it.

Pero Niño dismissed the men who had campaigned with him, and went to Valladolid where was his home. And although he was juſt back from the wars, he had made a livery of a ſtrange and particoloured fashion, and gave it to everyone who was in his house, great or small. Then he went to Madrid, where was the

King, and appeared at the Court armed, he and his gentlemen, like a man who for long had been continually at the wars in the service of his lord the king. He was very well received by the King and by all the Court; and the King, wishing to honour him and to recompense him for the services he had rendered, said to him : "Pero Niño, it is my wish that you should at once be made Knight." Pero Niño answered : "My lord, I might already have been dubbed Knight in other places and lands where I have been, and where other gentlemen were knighted according to the custom of the countries I have visited ; but, my lord, my desire was ever to receive this order of knighthood at your hands and in your house, for I am your creature, and of your favour was I nurtured. And if it were not that I now bear arms, I would have wished not to be made Knight, before you, my lord, set out with your army upon one of those conquests on which your noble heart is set ; but let it be done as your Grace commands." Then the King summoned all the great men of his Court, made a most noble feast, and there he dubbed the captain Knight ; and he said to him : "Pero Niño, my desire is to raise you to much higher estate and to send you on a conquest that shall be for you fair and honourable."

[1407] At this time there arrived the Ambassadors of France, Messire Robin and the Bishop of Saint-Flour. Already the King Don Enrique was seeking an opportunity and a means to make Pero Niño a

Grandee.[148] At this time war broke out against the Moors on account of the Castle of Ayamonte that the Moors had taken. The King left Madrid and went to Toledo, where he ordered all things for war. There he fell ill of a great sickness of which he died. A few days afterwards his son, the King Don Juan, was proclaimed King. Divisions soon arose in the realm, as happens whenever Kings are children in years. The grandees of the realm came together and went to the Court with many men whom they had in league with them to seize the King; and they wished to set the kingdom under the governance of Protectors. But the Infante Don Fernando, loyal and noble and a good Catholic, was then in Castille, who broke up all their intrigues. The Infante himself and the Queen Doña Catalina, mother of the King Don Juan, remained as the sole Regents of the kingdom, and maintained the realm in peace and justice and great quiet so long as they lived.

So soon as a good understanding was agreed between them, they resolved to continue the war against the Moors that had just been entered upon. They likewise decided to send Pero Niño and the Bishop of Leon as Ambassadors to France.

The Infante Don Fernando, uncle of the King, when he found himself Protector, had no thought but to take up again the war against the Moors at the point where the King Don Enrique, his brother, had left it. Then Pero Niño besought the Queen and the Infante as a favour that they should not send him to France at this time, although he would have gone there willingly, and it would have suited his plans because

of his business there ; but he gave up the journey
because it did not befit him to go on an embassy
in time of war, for he believed that in this war he
might render more service to God and to the King
than he could in the Embassy. The Regents were
pleased at Pero Niño's arguments and granted him
his request. And he, although he was but newly back
from the sea, established a troop of sixty men at arms,
all well armed and well mounted, each having two
horses and a coat of his livery, according to the usage
then newly brought in ; and there was not one of them
who had not a plumed crest. Then he sent a letter
to my Lady of Serifontaine.[149]

The Infante Don Fernando raised an army and went
into the kingdom of Granada. He entered it by way of
Moron and besieged Zahara, took it by force and seized
Torre Alhaquin, Pruna, and Ayamonte, which had
been lost and was the cause of this war. He likewise
took Cañete, Las Cuevas and Pego.[150] Pero Niño
was present at all these places that the Infante took,
and made better use of his hands than any man.
The Infante, when he had taken Zahara, marched on
Setenil. While the army was on the march, the
Constable Don Ruy Lopez departed from them with
two thousand horsemen, and went to reconnoitre
round Ronda, and took up a position before the city.
There were there rocks near a mosque and a little
bridge, and before the town there was a place called
the Little Market, that was full of Moors on foot and
mounted, who shot many arrows thence, and those

who were on horseback came and hurled their lances against the Constable's men, and then went back again. There befell a lively skirmish. The Constable did not let all his men take part therein, but Pero Niño was there mounted on a good horse and well armed, and he came away from the midst of the troop and was soon some way off with Ruy Diaz de Mendoza the Bald, who said to Pero Niño : " I know this country, and I will show you a good path by which you can go against the Moors." Ruy Diaz said this to see what he would do, and Pero Niño for his part desired to test his companion, who was rumoured to be a valiant knight and a good gentleman. Pero Niño was pressing forward with this intent, when the Constable came up to him and reasoned with him so much that he restrained him this time ; but before he had rejoined the troop the skirmish began again at close quarters. and Pero Niño returned to it with three or four of his men, for there were no more of them that had seen what was happening. As the Moors were on a height above an escarpment, between the rocks and the mosque, the knight and his horse, which bore no armour, found themselves closely pressed there. They hurled so many stones at them that the horse half-wheeled, whereat Pero Niño felt great displeasure and great shame, for never had might of enemies driven him back nor made him turn. And the horse, which was gallant and loyal, returned to the charge, feeling the will of its rider, and thrust itself into the midst of the Moors in such wise that their line was broken and that they took to flight towards the town. And let him know, who would know, that between **Pero Niño** and the Christians who were of his following there were more than a hundred Moors; and he went forward striking and killing, and as the place was strait, not a blow was lost. When he had broken his lance against them he drew his sword, and struck so many and such signal blows that it was all one whether those whom they reached were armed or not, for none of them used lance again.

Thus did he go as far as the bridge which is near to the city; then there came out a knight armed and on foot, who most boldly came up to him near enough to lay hands on his horse's reins. Pero Niño struck him such a blow on the top of the head, that he split his headpiece over his skull, and the Moor fell to the ground dead, but with the blow Pero Niño nearly lost his sword. In this hour he had to pass through perils and labours so great that no other knight in the world has ever had to face more in the same length of time; for the Moors had seized him by the legs, striving to drag him from his horse, and tore off the sheath of his sword and his dagger; but with the help of God he freed himself from them all in fine fashion; and whoever looked closely might see those who were above the gate leave the walls and fly towards the castle. Thus cutting his way, Pero Niño felt his horse weaken beneath him; and he looked and saw that it had lost much blood and could no longer bear him, and that his spurs availed him little. Then he turned the head of his horse, that had reached the end of its forces, towards his own men, and continued to strike and cut a way out of the midst of the Moors who were laying hands upon him. The horse came of a good stock; although strength failed it by reason of the great blows and wounds that it had received, its courage did not fail, and it got its master out of this pass. Before the horse fell, a page brought up another to Pero Niño, and a moment later the brave horse rolled dead to the ground, its entrails coming out of its belly.

Pero Niño set himself afresh to fight the Moors, and soon his second horse was covered with so many wounds that only with great difficulty could he get back to his men. The rider had been spared no more than the horse; only the blows fell upon good armour, though not so good but that it was broken and bent in many places. His sword was like a saw, toothed in great notches, the hilt twisted by dint of striking mighty blows, and all dyed in blood. Later Pero Niño sent this sword by a page to France, with other presents to my Lady of Serifontaine.

The Constable departed thence and rejoined the army. The Infante Don Fernando set up his camp before Sentenil and surrounded it on every side. Each day he assailed it with bombards which hurled stone cannon balls, and he wished to assault it. He had made a penthouse of strong wood covered with leather, and ordered Pero Niño to post himself with his men near the moats and to keep watch over the penthouse, to prevent the Moors from burning it. Pero Niño took this charge, and to fulfil it he and his men had to run great dangers and endure great weariness so long as the Infante remained there, for the Moors made surprise attacks from the town by night as by day, so that those who guarded the

PLATE VII

THE SIEGE

From a miniature of the Chronicle of Jerusalem illuminated for Philippe le Bon by " the master of the Girart de Roussillon." Vienna, Bibl. Imp., MS. 2533

penthouse could not for its defence either eat or sleep. Many were killed and wounded in these encounters. Pero Niño made some famous shots with the arbaleſt from behind the penthouse, for he was a good crossbowman.

One day the Infante ordered Pero Niño, Garcia de Valdés, and other knights, to creep below the rocks, to make a reconnaissance round the city as far as they could get, and to examine the moat and the foot of the ramparts to see if it were possible to make an assault. They set out well armed, covered by great shields, and went right round the city, receiving many ſtones and arrows ; then they came back to the Infante and told him that the whole city was set on the living rock, that was in some places lance-high, and in others six fathoms ; and that to reach the foot of the rock a very steep slope must be climbed. And these knights and others who were of their opinion said that the city could not be taken by assault.

. . .

After this the Infante ordered a tower to be made of wood, high and strong, well covered with leather and mounted on wheels ; and he ordered the Conſtable to have it brought out before the gate of the city, as that was the weakeſt point, although it was defended by a great tower which was above the gate. The entrance was barricaded and protected by a good moat which the Infante ordered to be filled in with faggots and sacks of earth. If they had heeded certain knights the city might have been taken, although it would have been a hard matter ; but a great party of knights of Caſtille set out to wreck the project,[151] because they

197

were ill content with the Infante, and did not yet hold
him in such fear and reverence as they were to do
later. One day when Pero Niño was in the penthouse, without saying anything to any of his men, he
went out armed with a coat of mail, with a cap, arm
pieces, a sword, and his buckler on his arm, and went
straight forward to the salient of the rampart, close
against the moat, examining everything quietly and
step by step, until he had come opposite the gate of the
city. There he got a handful of quarrells in his
buckler, and came back to the penthouse. Know
that during this course he received many attentions
from the Moors who were at the barricades of the
city; and he had hardly got back behind the penthouse before there fell upon it a hail of arrows and
stones, which lasted a long time. As the penthouse was roofed with hides, the noise was so great
that a man could not hear himself speak, and it sounded
as if the world were coming to an end in a storm.

The Infante learned what was going on and that
many of his men were deserting at night; he broke
camp very ill content and much against his will and
went off to Setenil. When he set out the best part
of the day was already over; he spent the night at
Olvera, and the Constable, the Master of St Iago, the
count Don Martin Vasquez de Acuña, Pero Niño and
other knights remained with the rear guard. This
breaking camp was done with so little care, that
they burnt one of the Infante's tents while firing some
huts, and they set out so late that they reached Olvera
at night. The Infante had ordered Pero Gongalez
de Baeza and Gonzalo Rodriguez de Ledesma to set

out with the siege equipment, and commanded them
to take it with a certain number of foot and horse to
Zahara. They were to go by New Ronda, between
Montecorte and Old Ronda. Almoſt as they left the
camp the great bombard, that took twenty pairs of
oxen to draw, overturned in the road, and likewise a
smaller bombard that could be drawn by a single pair
of oxen. The great bombard was altogether un-
mounted in its fall, and several pieces were loſt that
the Moors succeeded in taking. The Infante, when he
was told of what had happened, gave orders to certain
knights to go to the rear, to give support in that
quarter. They went thither ; but on the way some
of those that had joined them abandoned them. As
for them, they held firm as good knights should, and
sent to the Infante to ask for aid, telling him of the
great jeopardy in which they ſtood. Thereupon
the Infante made requeſt to several knights who were
about him, and even to some of his own household,
but each made some excuse. When the Infante saw
the affair in such peril, he had to send to warn the
Conſtable, who had scarcely been dismounted half
an hour and who was supping, to beg of him of his
kindness, for the love of God, for his duty and his
nobility, to go to the succour of those knights. This
appeared a serious matter to the Conſtable, to the
Count Martin Vasquez, to Pero Niño and to the other
knights who were there ; not because of the danger
they would run therein, but because the knights and
the other men had come up very weary, and their
horses had not yet eaten their oats and were not even
unbridled. But the good Conſtable, who was ever

wishful to show himself in such actions, and had taken
part in some of note, let it be apparent to those who
watched him that he wished to accept; and neither
the Count Martin Vasquez nor Pero Niño, nor any
of the knights who were there, were men to put
obstacles in his way. At once each of them ordered the
horses to be rested and groomed; but three hours
had not passed before the trumpets sounded to horse,
so that when the sun rose the Constable and those who
were there with him were before Setenil. They found
Moorish horsemen and footsoldiers outside the city,
whom they quickly drove in again by force. And the
Constable, who spoke Arabic, called for the Cadi, who
was captain[152] of the city. He showed himself to the
Constable and asked him what he had come to seek in
Setenil. " When the good King Alfonso came here ",
he said, " I was already captain, for I am more than
eighty years old. The King looked at Setenil and
examined it. Then the rock said to him ' Go hence ! '
and he went. If thou comest to seek for a little
iron, I have taken it to shoe my horses. If thou
comest to succour these Christians, it is true enough
that they are in great trouble ". The Constable
answered him that they were come for a certain task
that the Infante had ordered them to do, and he
dismissed him in the name of God. Then they went
forward a little and found the great bombard overturned, that there was no way of raising. At once
they began to mend its carriage and the other things
that might serve. They had been so occupied for
perhaps an hour when from the side of Olvera there
appeared about two hundred men at arms and four

or five hundred foot soldiers; and when these came near they saw that they were Diego Fernandez de Quiñones and Carlos de Arellano, who told him that they were come by order of the Infante to lend their aid. Discussing among themselves the task that each should undertake in this matter, brave words were exchanged between good knights. Finally these two knights bore off the small bombard which thirty men on foot could carry. These men gave their shields to others, and bound the bombard on to boughs and tree-trunks that they had cut; and bearing it went away along the path they had come by. The Conſtable with those in his company, ſtayed there to set up and carry off the great bombard, which took them more than four hours. They dragged it a very little way with great difficulty, for the ground was moſt uneven, and the bombard fell again three or four times. Each time it dragged the oxen with it, and to set it up again took more than an hour. During all this journey the good knight Pero Niño, although fully armed, conſtantly went afoot, directing and helping in the work, as occasion demanded, and never mounted his horse, although several times the news was spread that many Moors were coming up on foot and on horseback. He would not get into the saddle again until they had reached the height of Audita, where three roads divide, one to New Ronda, one to Old Ronda, and the third to Montecorto. The reſt of the siege train were then climbing a hill, and were in safety, for they were a good three leagues forward. There did the good knight Pero Niño and the Count Martin Vasquez ſtop with a hundred men at arms, until they thought that the siege train muſt have been more than three hours at Zahara, which took them well on into the night. Those who had done all this labour with the good Conſtable were about four hundred men at arms, with not a single foot-soldier. The look-outs had several times seen as many as two thousand Moorish horsemen and eight or ten thousand foot.

. . .

And so they drove back the Moors they encountered into their fortress, and saved the honour of Caſtille in not leaving the siege train in the hands of the enemy, and laboured all that day from dawn to sunset, surrounded by a multitude of enemies, shewing them that they were among those that love honour much. Thus the Infante departed from the kingdom of Granada, and after he had set all that concerned the war in order, he came to Guadalajara, where were the King and the Queen.

. . .

[1408] At this time Pero Niño was with the King and Queen, and there was entruſted to him one of the three captaincies of the King's guard ; and a hundred lances were given him, who were counted in his company, the King's guard being of three hundred lances. For this reason it was not possible for him to go to France. He sent to my lady to release him from his engagements to her, since he could not go himself. And this was right, so that so great a lady should not go on truſting in his return, as she had done heretofore, according to the agreement which I have earlier told.

HERE ENDS THE SECOND PART

202

THE THIRD PART

.   .   .

Pero Niño was at this time greatly renowned as a good knight, as well in battle as in jouſts and journeys, generous, enterprising, moſt brilliant in his equipment, diſtinguished at the palace and very courteous, which made him beloved of all the world. Men spoke well of him wherever he was known. Never could they bring the reproach againſt this knight that either in the palaces or in the houses he frequented did bitter words or disputes arise through his fault ; but the good renown of his aƈtions so told upon others that it drove them to desire to have to do with him. He was always temperate and courteous in his speech, having most careful regard to the person who drew him into conversation; he said that sharp words should be left to women, whose vice and cuſtom they were, and that men would do better to come to blows, which are their virtue and calling ; but no man ever cared about coming to blows with him.

[1409] The Infante Don Fernando at this time held great feſtivals and rejoicings at Valladolid, for the Queen of Navarre,[153] his aunt, was then come thither, and with her honourable knights and great lords, and many fair ladies and damsels. There were also there several knights, ambassadors of France and England, and Moors, ambassadors of Granada. And the Queen, the King's mother, often had jouſts held and tilting with canes, and tournaments on foot and on horseback, so that almoſt every day the knights jouſted, and Pero Niño was always among them. Ordinarily when he jouſted he took with him four or five knights of his household armed for the sport ; at other times he went alone, and jouſted with very strong lances, and each day had more than one encounter in which he overthrew many knights and these from among those who had emptied other men's saddles.

One day it fell out that they jouſted in a ſtreet which is called the *Cascagera*, where for the moſt part of the time they used to meet again and again, and Pero Niño jouſted that day. Among the knights that he threw to the ground was one of the moſt valiant and the moſt considerable of the Infante's household ; and this knight was of such a condition that his rank obliges me not to name him. In this ſtreet, there was an honourable mansion where at that time lodged the lady Doña Beatriz, daughter of the Infante Don Juan ; with her was Doña Margarida, her cousin, daughter of the Count Don Enrique Manuel.

And[154] there had several times been queſtion of the son of the Infante taking her to wife ; and she was of such condition, by reason both of her beauty and her birth, that it would have been, in faɛt, very fitting ; but his desire lay not in that quarter. The day that Pero Niño overthrew this great knight of the Infante's household, it happened, as ordinarily happens in such cases, that some had great displeasure and some great joy at his fall. And at that time the lady Doña Beatriz was looking on at what was happening in the jouſt, and with her her cousin Doña Margarida, and other ladies and damsels ; and Doña Margarida said : " It is no marvel that the knight falls when his horse falls ; the fault lies not with the rider but with the horse." Doña Beatriz made answer : " Cousin, you judge not well, nor do you say what you have in your thoughts. You have seen well enough, I think, that this knight has fallen because he bent beneath the weight of arms, and he has pulled so hard at the reins that horse and rider have both rolled to the ground." And moſt of the ladies and damsels who were there agreed with the lady Doña Beatriz. Other persons also were present at this conversation, and among them was a squire of Pero Niño's, to whom belonged the house in which Doña Beatriz was lodged ; and he told all to his lord, according as the ladies had judged.

In the time of which I am telling you, Pero Niño had already freed himself of his promise to my lady the Admiral's wife, the great lady of whom I have spoken before, whom he had loved when he was in France ; he had sent to take his leave of her, by reason of the war with the Moors ; and according to the agreement which had been made between them the time was already paſt for which she should await him and he should rejoin her, if it lay in his power, within the time that he had set.

And here the author says that things which are bound to happen, muſt happen and muſt have a beginning ; and that this was the occasion and the beginning of the marriage of these two, a marriage for which they both had to go through many and great trials. And while the squire was telling Pero Niño the words that Doña Beatriz has spoken, at that very moment the knight firmly resolved in his heart that he would love this damsel, to the advancement of his honour, and notwithſtanding that she was betrothed, for he underſtood that the marriage was too unequal for reasons of age. And at the same time Pero Niño learned how matters ſtood with Doña Beatriz, and that this barter that the Infante would have had her make had disposed her to accept no husband but one who pleased her. And juſt as Pero Niño used to adventure himself upon other great affairs so he adventured on this also. He discovered someone by whom to say to Doña Beatriz that she was the one lady in the world whom he would moſt desire to serve for his honour, and that he thought to vow himself thereto until death, for she was more noble than any of the queens of all Spain, that there was no damsel of fairer fame, nor of higher lineage ; and that he besought her to be pleased to allow him to call himself her knight, and he should show himself such in all due places.

And when she had liſtened to this embassy, she was much amazed and greatly troubled in her heart, and changed colour, and answered nothing to the messenger at that time. But Pero Niño did not cease from winning men over to him and from gaining the good will of those of whom he knew her to take counsel, and who were of her household and near her person. He did them much honour and gave them gifts, but without giving them any hint of his motive. Soon, of all the folk who were of the household of this lady, there was not one who did not speak of Pero Niño and of his noble exploits ; the truth is that he gave them matter enough for talking. The most part of them knew not all, although they guessed somewhat. And there was so much talk of him among all the household, that Doña Beatriz was amazed thereat; wherefore one day she called two of her maidens in whom she had great truſt, and said to them, "Tell me, friends, who has slipped into this household Pero Niño, a man to whom I have never spoken, whom I only know by hearsay? I see that everyone in this house talks of him and vaunts his deeds and his courtesy more than you do for any other knight of Caſtille." And one of them answered: "If he were not what he is, we should not thus praise him; but he is to-day, without queſtion, the flower of all knights in nobility and in chivalry, and in all fair virtues, as much as could be the beſt knight in the world." And the other said: "My lady, it is the truth, and there is even more good than one can say in him; and happy will be the woman who shall have such a husband and lord, for she shall be happy all her life and live in delight." And these damsels already knew how to speak well of him, for they had been prompted by this squire who spoke with them every day. And Doña Beatriz answered: "Ah, my friends, how you deceive yourselves! I know well that he is to-day one of the moſt famous knights in the world; but they tell me that great ladies have loſt their good name for his sake, and I would not myself be numbered among them; well do ye know that it is the thing from which I have ever kept myself the moſt, and I order that ye never let me hear another word on this head." Such was her answer that day; and the squire bore it to

Pero Niño. But he, who never forgot what he had resolved in his heart, took much thought to find a way to tell her all, face to face. One day, when she set out from her lodging to ride, he contrived to be in her path, and to be asked by those who were there to take the reins of her horse ; and he did so, for it was the chance he sought, and luck sent it him at that moment. And so walking at her side, he had leisure to disclose to her all his intent, reminding her how he had already made them known to her, and beseeching her to be well assured that his desire was to love her uprightly and loyally, to the honour of them both. She answered that men's words should always be mistrusted, but that she would take the advice of those who were bound to counsel her loyally, and that then she would give him his answer.

Pero Niño did not cease from searching out the best means of bringing the affair to a head. And the lady Doña Beatriz had a brother, the natural son of her father the Infante Don Juan, who was called Don Fernando, a good knight and a close friend of Pero Niño's in time past. During the time that Doña Beatriz took to give him an answer, Pero Niño declared himself to Don Fernando, her brother, and told him all his thoughts and the points at which matters were. When Don Fernando knew this, he showed himself greatly pleased thereat and promised Pero Niño his help, understanding that it would be to his sister's honour, after all the marriages that had been projected for her, and the intrigues that had been carried on in the household of my lord the Infante. Forthwith Don Fernando went to his sister, on behalf

PLATE VIII

THE MEETING

From a miniature of the Histoire de Charles Martel. Brussels, Bibliothèque Royale de Belgique, MS. 7, fol. 204v

[*Photo. Vromont*]

of Pero Niño, and they talked together of things
paſt, present and to come ; and over these laſt they
lingered longeſt, for they would have to be accomplished without the leave of my lord the Infante,
who was at the moment in the King's ſtead, for he was
Regent of the realm during the minority of the King
his nephew.

Returning to Pero Niño, he recounted all that had
been said, how he had made remonſtrance with Doña
Beatriz of the toils and troubles which might arise
therefrom and the perils which would follow ; saying
that if he would go on with it to the end, she for her
part was resolved likewise, according to the advices
of her brother and of others who gave her loyal
counsel, having regard to his chivalry ; for Pero Niño
was such a man as would bring the matter to a sure end,
and there was not in all the realm ? knight to whom
it should pertain to undertake such an enterprise, if
it were not to him.

At all this Pero Niño rejoiced greatly when he heard
this answer, for with great wisdom he had already
looked upon himself in the mirror of high prudence,
and had seen that he was bound to all these adventures
and to as many others as might befall. The marriage
was thus concerted by Doña Beatriz' brother and by
other persons in authority, and the betrothal was
celebrated by a prieſt, in the presence of these discreet
and honourable persons ; and pledges, dowries, and
bonds of towns and vassals, as befitted such a lady,
were assigned him before men who cherished his honour
and were bound to consider the intereſts of both
parties, to serve them and to keep their secret until

the day when it should be declared, although several among them had much trouble already of mind concerning the persecutions that might follow. However, as they saw the matter arranged by the principals, they thought that all would end well, and that such was the will of God, as in fact was seen later.

And henceforward Pero Niño was much more joyous than he had been hitherto, and maintained his household in readier array and on a larger footing, as a man who thought to bring this affair to a head. And henceforward he took little heed to keep it secret ; to some he spoke of it, and to others who questioned him, he did not deny it, so that he knew that it had been spoken of to the Infante, and before the matter went further he wished to tell him thereof himself. Now as the lord Infante desired to make war, and especially against the Moors, he gave him a warmer welcome than to any other knight of his rank or above it, and Pero Niño came to find him and said to him : " My lord, I have been brought up by the King Don Enrique your brother, and as your grace knows, I have done him good service both by land and sea ; and at the time when he proposed to give me recompense and high estate, according to his promise, God took him from this world. It is true that as your Grace was there, I thought that your Grace would reward and recompense the services that I had done to his Grace the King your brother, and likewise do I intend to serve you as well as any knight can who serves King or lord, for which, thanks be to God, I am well prepared. At this time, my lord, it is fitting that I should take a wife, and I am proposed some of the greateſt matches in the kingdom ; but as I have the intent to serve you better than all the kings in the world and as I would be altogether yours, I would rather marry into your household."

The Infante answered him : " All that you say is truth, and you should reſt assured that in all matters wherein I can help you I will give you aid as to the man whom I hold neareſt to me, who serves in my household. Let it please you then to tell me who is in queſtion and where your inclination lies." Then Pero Niño answered that he was somewhat embarrassed to speak of it himself, but that he would make answer through the Infante's Confessor, and the Infante said that it was well.

On the morrow Pero Niño went to the Confessor, and reported to him the speech between himself and the Infante. He revealed to him that the damsel was Doña Beatriz, daughter of the Infante Don Juan. This appeared somewhat diſturbing[55] to the Confessor, for he knew that the Infante was considering other marriages for the lady outside the realm of Caſtille, and even that he had not altogether rejeĉted the projeĉt of a marriage with his son. None the less he promised that he would give the message and report the answer. And before two or three days had passed Pero Niño had his answer through the Confessor : and the answer was that the Infante ordered him and besought him not to speak further of this marriage, for he had already negotiated and arranged a marriage elsewhere, which it was moſt important should be made, and which it was no longer possible

to break ; but he pressed him to caſt his eyes round all
the kingdom for the match which would otherwise be
the moſt to his liking, and he would second him in this
as he had promised, and thereat would be rejoiced
greatly. Pero Niño made answer to the Confessor
that he might know for certain that if he did not wed
this lady, all his life he would wed no other, and that
if the Infante, so assured, would grant him this grace,
he would make him the happieſt knight in the world
and would soon see this in his services ; but that if he
refused it him, he would rather be beheaded. The
Confessor replied that to please him he would report
their talk, although the Infante had spoken to him
about it very ſternly.

From that time Pero Niño considered himself
discharged, because of what he had made known to the
Infante. To speak truth, he perceived at once
what troubles were about to befall him, and henceforward he guarded himself more closely than he had
done heretofore. He went everywhere on horseback,
for he was the beſt mounted man in the kingdom, and
he ever kept round him twenty to thirty knights and
squires, well equipped and provided with good
horses. Marten robes were no longer often seen ; the
coat of mail was his ordinary apparel.

.   .   .

One night Pero Niño was at the palace with the
King and Queen. The King had come thither from
Magaz, where he then used commonly to live, and
Pero Niño with him, since he was one of the chiefs of
his guards. As his affairs went forward, each day
finding him more closely pressed, he had had to come

to see his betrothed, and, as a knight should, maintain the enterprise wherein his honour was at stake. So, when he reached the palace, the Infante had him summoned to his chamber, where were the Bishop of Palencia and the Constable, to learn from his lips the truth of the matters concerning which there was so much talk. The Infante told him that he must remember how the question had already been raised between them, and how through his Confessor he had begged and commanded him not to speak a word of this marriage and to renounce it, but now that he had been warned that he pretended to have espoused Doña Beatriz; and that on this point he wished to know from his own lips how matters stood.

Pero Niño made answer: " My lord, your Grace knows well that when your Confessor bade me speak no more of this matter, and to renounce it, I answered that it was not a thing which I could in any wise give up; that I thought to be within my rights, and that this marriage would be agreeable to your Grace for several reasons : first, because if God had so disposed matters that our two hearts were of one accord, it was a case in which no man should interpose to set impediment ; secondly, that I thought myself a knight of such standing as to merit Doña Beatriz, having done you signal service with my person, and being to-day ready to serve you still, as well as any knight that is in the world ; and that I asked you as a favour, beseeching you as well as I could, to consent to grant me this, whereby you would make me the happiest knight in the world ; and that otherwise I would prefer death."

Thereupon were many words spoken, that it would

213

take long to tell, and at once Pero Niño departed
thence for Magaz. Many of those who were in the
palace thought that Pero Niño would be arreſted
forthwith, but he was not. He had spoken so wisely
and had put forward so many good arguments in his
favour, and had expressed them with such courage,
and the Infante was so noble and so inclined to juſtice,
that he did not have him arreſted ; and if there had not
been evil counsellors, he would assuredly have granted
his consent.

Little time passed ere the Infante and the Infanta
sent for Doña Beatriz, and in the presence of the
Bishop, asked her if it were true that Pero Niño was
her husband, as he said. She at firſt had great fear
leſt Pero Niño should have been arreſted, knowing
that he was at that time in the Infante's palace ; but
she heard from a squire that he had again departed.
She answered that such was indeed the truth. And
they asked her how she had dared do such a thing
againſt the wish of the Infante, when it was a queſtion
of her marriage with his son ; that she had committed
a hideous wrong. She brought forward to defend
herself many reasons which had moved her to do this
thing ; one of them was that the Infante well knew
that before he was Regent in Caſtille, in the lifetime
of the King his brother, he had betrothed her to his
son, but that later, after he had become Regent of the
realm, he had considered other marriages for her
abroad, some honourable, others less so ; wherefore
she had resolved in her heart to marry no man but
someone she should love. She added that several of
her kinsmen, and others who were intereſted in her

honour, had presented this knight to her, that she had betrothed herself to him, and counted herself fortunate. She said that she besought the Infante to approve him ; that this would be a great favour to her ; that she had done what she ought, and that she was assured that she had chosen a knight of such a sort and so good that the Infante could promise himself that he would be well served.

The Infante answered that she must speak no more of consent, and that of necessity she had prepared great troubles for herself. She replied that she was prepared to bear all the troubles that might come to her from this cause ; and thereupon the Infante ordered her not to return to her lodging, but to remain with the Infanta her cousin.

On the morrow the Infante sent the Bishop of Segovia and Pedro de Monsalvo, the King's treasurer, to the Queen, who was with the King at Magaz, to lodge information with her against Pero Niño, saying that he had betrothed himself to Doña Beatriz when she was already betrothed to the Infante's son. Upon which they brought forward many arguments why Pero Niño should be arrested and why the Queen should deliver him up to be imprisoned. The Queen had long known everything and favoured Pero Niño ; but she had not enough of might or boldness to do as much as she would have liked to do. She caused the knight to appear forthwith before the ambassadors. There he declared in truth that he had betrothed himself to Doña Beatriz, and he gave the reasons therefor. He said further : " The Infante is not my master ; if he bear me ill will, and if, in his household, there are some to whom what I have done is displeasing, who pretend that I have incurred reproach and wish to maintain this, I will fight them before the King my master, before the Queen and the Infante, and under the eyes of Doña Beatriz my wife. Let them choose two from among them, whomsoever the Infante wills, or whomsoever they choose themselves, and I will give them satisfaction according as the law of knights decrees in such a case, holding the field from one sunrise until the next. I will vanquish them one by one ; when I have dispatched the one, in whatever plight I may be, I will fight the other without respite, and I will kill them, or make them leave the field, or oblige them to confess that I have done no wrong in betrothing myself to my wife Doña Beatriz, and that she likewise is in no wise to be blamed." The condition that he set was that when the fixed time had elapsed and after the conflict to which he proposed himself, the King should make him, in the presence of all, remitment of his wife, free and quit of all recovery. Moreover, at the end of his discourse, he added that he offered to give the knights who should accept his challenge two thousand doubloons each for their horses.[156]

The ambassadors left him, bearing this challenge with the Queen's consent, and went to seek the Infante; but they were not slow in returning, and on the morrow they brought back the answer : that they would not grant him this favour, but would set the affair in order in a manner more troublesome for him. And at once they began to treat with the Queen concerning his arrest, saying that otherwise the Infante would come in person. The Queen ſtill feared to have all power over the King her son taken away from her; she therefore called Pero Niño and told him that she well knew how he had served the King Don Enrique and the King her son; that she had knowledge of all the toils he had endured and endured every day to guard and defend the King, but that the Infante might come to Magaz and there have him arreſted; whereat, said she, she would have great grief not being able to prevent it, and that for this reason she besought him to withdraw to the Alcazar of Palenzuela, of which caſtle Pero Niño was then captain for the King, and that in the meantime she would do all she could in his favour. Pero Niño, having heard the Queen, and seeing that she could do no more, departed thence and went to Palenzuela, where he remained for some days.

The Infante, on the very day that Pero Niño left Magaz, has sent to him at Villamediana, where he was lodging, Diego Fernandez de Badillo, to find out what course he was taking. Pero Niño had everything reported to him by Diego Fernandez and haſtened to get to Palenzuela. The Infante had sent out men to lay hands on him, and some were in certain places that Pero Niño passed through, but they did not dare to attack him, and he was able to get to Palenzuela. He had been there three days when the Queen sent to him Rodrigo de Perea, Adelantado of Cazorla, and Garcia Furtado, a sergeant crossbowman of the King's, to ask him and command him to go thence, binding him to withdraw to Bayonne in Gascony, for she could not proteĉt him. By this knight Rodrigo de Perea, serving in the household of the King and a

man of credit, and by Garcia Furtado, crossbowman,
also servant and officer in the King's household, the
Queen sent him a letter, for the law decreed that no
gentleman should leave the kingdom without incurring
accusation, unless it were by the King's command, or
for some juſt cause of renouncing their fealty; wherefore it was necessary that Pero Niño should receive
such a command; otherwise he could not have
departed.

Here we cease speaking of him and of his journey
to Bayonne, in which he had to endure many toils
and dangers, to talk of his wife, the lady Doña Beatriz.

Doña Beatriz had been kept in the palace of the
Infante, who sought to hold her, sometimes by fear,
and sometimes by gentleness, bidding her give up
Pero Niño, and he would at once find her better
matches in Caſtille. But she remained always firm
and conſtant againſt threats and prayers, answering
that she would never have any other husband than
Pero Niño, and that rather than give him up she would
suffer death, if she muſt. Thence the Infante sent her
to Urueña, and with her ladies and damsels to bear her
company and honourable service; there was she
honourably intreated, but closely guarded, so that no
man could get admitted to have speech with her, for
fear that Pero Niño should carry her off. During a
year and a half that she was there Pero Niño none the
less came and succeeded in seeing her. The three or
four times that he came, he might have carried her

off ; but he wished neither to carry her off nor to possess her, save in all honour, as it befell later.

While Pero Niño was at Bayonne, some knights who were his friends spoke to the Infante, and the Queen took a hand therein, as well as others who addressed themselves to the Infante's conscience, remonstrating with him on many counts : that such a knight was not to be loſt; that they might seek in many places without finding many as good as Pero Niño ; and likewise that he would be made welcome in other kingdoms, if he would remain there, and that the Infante had great need of him because of the war that he was then waging againſt the Moors. And for all these reasons and for others which moved him, the Infante consented to pardon him, and gave him permission to come back into the kingdom of Caſtille, gave him back to his wife, granted him other favours and compensations ; and in the end found ways to attach him to himself. If the Infante had lived longer, Pero Niño would have gone far with him. And when Pero Niño came back to Caſtille, the Queen accorded him many favours, re-eſtablished him in his rank and gave back to him the King's guard, as he had had beforetime. Pero Niño celebrated his marriage in one of his cities that is called Cigales. Henceforward, until the King's majority, he continued to follow the Court, where many things befell after the Infante Don Fernando died, being King of Aragon ; and in all these matters Pero Niño bore himself as nobly as he had always done.

.   .   .

NOTES

The sign   .   .   .   indicates an omission in the text.

C.P. indicates Comte A. de Circourt and Comte de Puymaigre, *Le Victorial, Chronique de don Pedro Niño, Comte de Buelna par Gutierre Diaz de Gamez son Alferez*, 1379-1449, *traduit de l'Espagnol d'après le manuscrit avec une introduction et des notes historiques.* Paris, Palmé, 1867, in 8vo.

Llaguno indicates Eugenio de Llaguno Amirola, *Cronica de Don Pedro Niño, Conde de Buelna, por Gutierre Diez de Games su Alferez*, Madrid, de Sancha, 1782, in 4to.

For biographical notes of all the persons mentioned the reader is referred to C.P.

1 The division of mankind into those who pray, those who fight, and those who labour is here probably taken from tit. 21, preamble, of the second of the *Siete Partidas* of Alfonso the Learned.

2 *Miseria.*

3 The etymology and account of *fidalgo* is taken from tit. 21, law 2, of the Second *Partida.*

4 The examples of bravery given have some analogy with the " Neuf Preux" of the *Vœux du Paon* of Jacques de Longuyon, two of the three classical heroes, Alexander and Caesar, having already been dealt with (C.P., pp. 18 and 30). Hector is omitted ; Charles Martel takes the place of Arthur ; and four Spanish examples are cited to make up the number.

5 *Apantasmas è apóstatas. Fantasma* has the secondary meaning of a person who gives himself airs.

6 *Esculcas, escuchas, atalayas, atajadores, algareros.*

7 The family is said to have received the surname of Niño because two of its orphaned heirs were brought up in the king's household and called by him the *niños* or children.

8 Cf. the rhymed *Chronicle of the Cid*, where Diégo Laynez counsels his son :
   " Al rey que vos servides, servillo muy sin arte.
   Assy vos aguardat dél como de enemigo mortal." (ll. 375-6).

9 Enrique II.

10 *Escudados :* men who bore the great shields or small penthouse which provided shelter for the crossbowmen.

11 *Armaba muy fuertes ballestas à cinto* ; C.P. translate as " arbalètes à pied-de-biche ", and are probably right, as this was the best crossbow

221

for the use of the mounted knight, as it was both comparatively light and ſtrong. For a drawing and a clear account of it, see Viollet le Duc, *Dictionnaire raissonné du mobilier français*, Paris 1874, Vol. V, p. 33.

[12] *Juego de viras ;* the *viras* were small quarrells only used for shooting at a mark.

[13] *Graciosas cantigas è saborosos dezires è notables motes è baladas è chazas* (?) *è rondelas è lays è virolais è complayntas è sonjes* (?) *è sonhays è figuras.*

[14] *Amor, dilecion, querenzia.*

[15] *Bien animallados :* this word is a coinage of Gamez' own.

[16] *Alieres,* quartermaſters who served under the orders of the pilot and the overseer. *Espaldepeles,* oarsmen who manned the oars of the firſt bench towards the poop ; they made the forward ſtroke. *Corullales,* oarsmen who manned the oars of the laſt bench, *corulla.* They made the backing ſtroke. See Jal, *Glossaire nautique,* s.v.

[17] I have usually translated *nao* as " sailing ship " : It was a round-hulled vessel high in the side, which chiefly depended on its sails.

[18] *Patron :* the chief naval officer of a ship.

[19] *Comitre ;* in a galley, " overseer " or " maſter of the oarsmen " ; in a sailing ship, " mate ".

[20] Such *Vœux du Paon, du Faisan,* or *du Heron* were the cuſtomary ending for a great knightly feaſt. The moſt famous are the "Vœux du Faisan " made at Lille in 1454 by Philippe le Bon of Burgundy and his knights, when preparing for Crusade.

[21] *Zabra.* The word seems to have been used indifferently for ships of considerable size and for small boats.

[22] *Atayferes.*

[23] *Tarazana.*

[24] *Atavales.*

[25] *Artimones :* the sails of the fore maſt of galleys ; the *artimones* were the sails used in bad weather.

[26] Peter de Luna, the Anti-Pope Benedict XIII.

[27] Llaguno *gruesas,* C.P. *ginosas.*

[28] *Fizo sala.*

[29] *Tinel.*

[30] *Calaron timones de caxa.* See Jal, *Glossaire nautique,* s.v. He supposes that they were set to port and ſtarboard of the rudder in bad weather.

NOTES

[31] *E con la grand fuerza de las olas, trocaronse los timones de caxa :*
I suppose they came unpinned from the sockets.

[32] *Escandelar :* one of the cabins of the ship.

[33] *Los marineros alzaron un poco las velas, entraron las pujas, é ficieron braguerotes á la vela, é entraron la osta é la sosta, é pusieron dos omes á las betas á ayudar, é ficieron cataldo para amaynar á fuerza del viento.* This manœuvre is discussed in detail in Jal,. loc. cit.

[34] *A orza :* in the Mediterranean the command to come into the wind is *Orza.*

[35] *Preles.*

[36] *Cabrayra.*

[37] *Lorbo.*

[38] *Ventosardo.*

[39] *Gemol, Gemolin :* C.P. state that the Catalan fourteenth century map published by Buchon gives the first island as Xmal, which is close to Gamez' transliteration.

[40] The channel of the Goulette.

[41] Alfonso the Catholic.

[42] Llaguno : *Bona de Buxia.*

[43] *Alquiceres.*

[44] *Los bastardos é las mezañas.* The *bastardo* was the great sail of the galley; the *mezaña* the mizzen sail; both were fair-weather sails.

[45] *Alhavina.*

[46] *Palomas, buldrejas, é alcatraces, é gaviotas, é falcones, é codornices.* C.P. propose to emend to *buedrejas,* diminutive of *buytre.*

[47] *Aquel aduar Arzeo que buscaban :* C.P. suggest that Arzeo is an interpolation of the copyist as both Old and New Arzeo are on the sea-shore and not two leagues inland as was the village that they looked for.

[48] *Alhorma* (from *haram*) the smala.

[49] *La gente aforrada,* who can move freely.

[50] *Alhombras :* Cañes, *Dict. hispan.-arabigo,* describes an *Alfombra* as a large carpet woven in one piece, made of silk and wool of many colours, usually with red predominating; and an *Alcatifa* as an *alfombra* with a heavier pile.

[51] *Copano pavesado.*

[52] C.P. suggest that the apparent contradiction between the West wind mentioned here and the fact that a few lines lower, going N.W., they had to row against the wind, is solved by the fact that off the

coaſt of Oran weſterly squalls are often heralded by a breeze from the Eaſt. See Bérard, *Description des côtes de l'Algérie*, p. 65.

53 *El Bergelete.* Neither this nor the caves of Alcocevar are marked on modern maps, but they probably correspond with the indications *Arcozava* and *Aqua oiva* on the fourteenth century Catalan map published by Buchon. The only grotto between Cape Falcon and Cape Tegalo (where Alcocevar muſt lie) is said to be the Ghar Debâa, at the foot of the Djebel Touila. (See C.P., pp. 554 sqq.)

54 *Non se escusaban de non correr de luengo.*

55 *Concertaron las brujelas cebadas con la piedra yman.*

56 *Al quartel de proa.*

57 The Bay of Biscay.

58 *La coſta de Valancina:* the coaſt of France between Bordeaux and Bayonne.

59 *Que hera la mar de canto :* the passage appears to be corrupt in both MSS.

60 MSS. *todas las islas ;* but there are no islands here.

61 *Las Aguas,* but it should read (as it does later in the text), *Las Asnas,* that is, the bar of the Gironde, where there is the channel of the Pas-des-Anes.

62 *Roanete, Talamon.*

63 *Mosen Charles de Savasil.* He had held the office of chief cup-bearer and firſt chamberlain to Charles VI, but, having maltreated a king's officer who had come to arreſt one of his servants, charged with robbery and murder, and having figured in a town-and-gown row in Paris, he was, at the inſtance of the Rećtor of the University, banished from the court and deprived of his offices. (See Monſtrelet, Chapter XIII ; Southey, *British Admirals*, p. 22.)

64 *Ir à buscar à Uxente.*

65 *Olona è Lairon* (?) *è por la villa de Garranca* (?).

66 *Samaïgo.* The identification is confirmed by the account of Savoisy's voyage in the chronicle of the *Religieux de Saint Denis.*

67 The English Channel

68 Llaguno *Lamua.* C.P. *La Mira.* C.P. consider it a place name ; I think it may simply be a watch-tower on the coaſt near Sluys.

69 *Brancharte.*

70 *Reposaron al algarete faſta el quarto del alba.* C.P. found no precedent for *algarete,* but considered it might have been a name for the watch from midnight to four o'clock that had fallen out of use ; or

else to have indicated that the ship rode at a small anchor that gave with the current.

[71] Llaguno, *el patron ;* MS. *el aleman.* C.P. suggeſt that this may indicate the man who observes the compass, *el iman.*

[72] *Oes sud ueſte ;* C.P. emend, on the ground that the galleys were going Weſt North Weſt and had the wind *por medio de las proas.*

[73] *Clucheres.*

[74] *Violartes :* this word has fallen out of use, but its meaning can be guessed.

[75] Possibly Hayle-mouth.

[76] *Chita.* C.P. suggeſt that this is St Erth, on one of the tributaries of the Hayle River ; but this seems unlikely. The description well fits St Ives, especially if it is remembered that the harbour there has begun to silt up again in modern times.

[77] A pavisade is ſtriⱳly a defence of a very close trellis, but is here and elsewhere in the *Vitorial* the usual shelter made by the Escudados.

[78] *Araflor.*

[79] *Alamua.* The identification is made certain, since it was at Dartmouth that Guillaume du Chaſtel was killed.

[80] *Guillen del Caſtel.*

[81] *Plamua.*

[82] Gamez probably means the rocks off Start Point. The Casquets, between Guernsey and Alderney, are clearly not in queſtion.

[83] *Porlan.*

[84] *Pola.*

[85] *Arripay.*

[86] Here, as on other occasions, Gamez tries to make Savoisy talk French : " *Monseñor, y faota que vos me perdoneis.*"

[87] *Antone.*

[88] It is evident that the sailors palmed off Southampton as London, in order to avoid a dangerous voyage.

[89] *Artamisa.*

[90] *Isla Duy.*

[91] *Moſterviller.*

[92] *Charruas.*

[93] *Tafurcas.*

[94] *Traense mucho à lo proprio.*

[95] *Dan posada à los enojosos.*

[96] *Mosen Arnao de Tria.*

[97] *Xirafontayna.*

NOTES

⁹⁸ *Bahanones:* The word is not Spanish, and may represent *Behaignon,* or Bohemian horse. It was in any case a jousting horse.

⁹⁹ *Javalies.*

¹⁰⁰ *Lays è deslays è virolays è chazas (?) è reondelas è complaintas baladas, chançones de toda el arte que troban los franceses.*

¹⁰¹ C.P. emend *turena* to *terrena.*

¹⁰² *Rodear señuelos.*

¹⁰³ Charles VI.

¹⁰⁴ The Dukes of Orleans, Burgundy, Berri and Bourbon.

¹⁰⁵ *Varas.*

¹⁰⁶ *Aventureros.*

¹⁰⁷ The *Petite Bretagne* was near the Louvre.

¹⁰⁸ *Muchas dansas e casaotes e chantarelas.*

¹⁰⁹ *Un varil escudo.*

¹¹⁰ The Culture, Coulture or Cousture Sainte Catherine du Val des Ecoliers.

¹¹¹ *Plançones.*

¹¹² This is a fair specimen of Gamez' notion of writing French.

¹¹³ Jean Bouciquaut in 1399 had founded an informal order " de la Dame-Blanche à l'écu vert " and this may possibly have some reference to it.

¹¹⁴ *Mosen Arnao Guillen de Baruasayn, Chapaña, Chuet de Braban, Argenbaoch, Carrogier, è Mosen Guillen Bataller.*

¹¹⁵ Lla. Chipre.

¹¹⁶ MSS. *de la Oga ;* Llaguno, *de la Heva.*

¹¹⁷ *Sulamer :* the identification is doubtful.

¹¹⁸ *San Gaittier.*

¹¹⁹ *La fosa de Cayo.* The Fosse-à-Cayeux, a creek near Cayeux sur mer, was navigable up to the eighteenth century.

¹²⁰ *Veralnorte.*

¹²¹ Southey suggests that the flying fishes are a memory of the Mediterranean, wrongly transferred to the North Sea.

¹²² *Oriola.*

¹²³ It is, in fact, three leagues.

¹²⁴ Llaguno *Francia.*

¹²⁵ Edward III took Calais in 1347, fifty-nine years before.

¹²⁶ Southey considered *Nuleta* equivalent to Nieulay, but this is too close to Calais and was in Pero Niño's time in English hands. C.P. suggests *Auletas,* for Ambleteuse, but agree that some place to the

North of Calais is more probable, though they cannot suggest an identification.

[127] *Fizo un fermoso loh ; quando vio que le cayen los navios de los Ingleses juslone tomo el viento en popa.*

[128] *E aun el ballener salio bien esgarrochado de entre los otros.*

[129] Philippa, daughter of Henry IV, betrothed to the King of Denmark, set out in September, 1406, from King's Lynn for Denmark.

[130] *Grevelingas.*

[131] *La Bahia.*

[132] *Libuxieres.*

[133] *Jarrasuy.*

[134] *Eĉtor de Ponprianes è el señor de Tornamira.*

[135] *Pillartes.*

[136] *Eĉtandartes.*

[137] *Llaguno : e correr mucho gente.*

[138] MSS. *Junques ;* a copyist's error for *jaques.*

[139] *Tablanchas.*

[140] *Pramua.*

[141] C.P. ingeniously suggest that this jargon is a more or less phonetic transcription of " Many years and good give you God and (to) each (of you)."

[142] Samalo de Lilla.

[143] *Ventaba aquel dia vent-a-mute ques viento del norte.*

[144] In the Straits of Messina.

[145] The Bay of Biscay and the Channel.

[146] *La Valancina.*

[147] *Mosen Robin de Bracamonte . . . Sanflor.*

[148] *Fazer grande honbre à Pero Niño.*

[149] *Madama la Almiralla de Francia.*

[150] Las Cuevas, Pego, Pruna, Ayamonte and Cañete form a girdle of caĉtles round Setenil.

[151] MSS. *ficieronlo maña ;* Llaguno, *ficieronlo mañera guerra.*

[152] *Alcaide.*

[153] Doña Leonora, daughter of Enrique II and wife of Charles III of Navarre.

[154] There is here a lacuna in both texts : evidently it concerned the marriage projeĉted between Doña Beatriz and the son of the Infante.

[155] *Un poco escuro.*

[156] The sum appears excessive to C.P., who suggeĉts two hundred doubloons.

INDEX

Of Names and Places

228

INDEX

229

INDEX

INDEX

INDEX